Y0-BCO-338

THE GREAT TORCH RACE

Essays in Honor of Reginald Harvey Griffith

WALTER BARNES STUDIO

Reginald Harvey Griffith

THE GREAT TORCH RACE

Essays in Honor of Reginald Harvey Griffith

Edited by Mary Tom Osborne

PUBLISHED FOR THE CONFERENCE OF
COLLEGE TEACHERS OF ENGLISH OF TEXAS
AND THE HUMANITIES RESEARCH CENTER OF
THE UNIVERSITY OF TEXAS BY THE
UNIVERSITY OF TEXAS PRESS · AUSTIN

LIBRARY OF CONGRESS CATALOG CARD NO. 61–10425

PRINTED IN THE UNITED STATES OF AMERICA
BY THE PRINTING DIVISION OF THE UNIVERSITY OF TEXAS

TABLE OF CONTENTS

THE GREAT TORCH RACE

Essays in Honor of Reginald Harvey Griffith

INTRODUCTION

REGINALD HARVEY GRIFFITH, in whose honor this volume has been compiled, died in Austin, Texas, on December 10, 1957. His had been a long life, rich in scholarly achievements and in service to fellow scholars, to students, to The University of Texas, and to Texas education in general.

Dr. Griffith was born in Charlotte, North Carolina, on February 3, 1873, the son of Richard Henry and Mary Ann (Coleman) Griffith. His father, a Baptist minister, was a leader of the Baptist church in the Carolina region and, for a number of years, was associated with Furman University as its financial agent. In 1906 Dr. Griffith married Alice Mary Matlock. Her death preceded his by several years. They had three children: a son, Richard Henry, who died in infancy, and two daughters, Helvetia Regina, now Mrs. R. Cazaris, of California, and Mary Nell, now Mrs. R. H. Guelich, of New York and California.

After preparatory work at the Greenville Military Institute, Dr. Griffith entered Furman University, where he received the degree of Master of Arts in 1892, at nineteen years of age. The next ten years were devoted chiefly to teaching in the public schools of North and South Carolina, with one year as Professor of English at Furman University and two years (1894–1896) of graduate study at Johns Hopkins University. After periods of research in the Harvard University Library and the British Museum, he moved from Johns Hopkins to the University of Chicago, where, in 1905, he received the Ph.D.

Three years earlier, in 1902, he had joined the faculty of The University of Texas as an instructor in the Department of English, beginning an association that was to continue for more than fifty years. In 1908 he was promoted to adjunct professor; in 1914, to associate professor; in 1919, to professor; and in 1925, to membership in the graduate faculty. In 1918 he was appointed curator of the newly acquired Wrenn Library. As research professor for the year 1935–1936 he delivered the customary three public lectures growing out of the year's study. In 1942, as he approached the age of seventy, he accepted modified service, continuing in this status until 1951, when he became professor emeritus. Following his retirement, Dr. Griffith set out for England, and from this time until traveling became a burden, he alternated between research libraries of England and America, making Austin—

and The University of Texas—his nominal home. He continued his scholarly activities through personal conferences, wide correspondence, and occasional notes in learned journals.

Various honors came to Dr. Griffith during his long career: in 1910 he was appointed a member of the Board of Visitors to the United States Naval Academy; in 1925 he received from Furman University the degree of Doctor of Letters; and in 1929 he was elected to Phi Beta Kappa.

Although Dr. Griffith was never for long separated from The University of Texas, he frequently accepted invitations to teach in summer sessions at other universities. In 1922, 1932, and 1945, he taught at the University of Chicago; in 1926, at the University of Colorado; in 1930, at Columbia University; in 1937, at Duke University.

Throughout forty years of full-time teaching at The University of Texas, Dr. Griffith, while carrying a heavy teaching load and, after 1925, directing theses and dissertations, consistently pursued his own research. He contributed significant articles to scholarly publications and, in 1940, helped with the revision of the *Cambridge Bibliography of English Literature.* His first published book was his doctoral dissertation, *Sir Percival of Galles: A Study of the Sources of the Legend,* a definitive work on this medieval subject. In 1924, the centennial of Byron's death, in connection with an exhibit of Byron's works set up at The University of Texas, he, with Howard Mumford Jones, compiled and published *A Descriptive Catalogue of an Exhibition of Manuscripts and First Editions of Lord Byron.*

His crowning work, the culmination of long years of dedicated study, was *Alexander Pope: A Bibliography, Volume I, Part I,* published in 1922, *Part II,* in 1927. As Professor Louis Landa states: "There is no question that the *Bibliography* is a magnificent scholarly accomplishment, that it must be known by any informed scholar in the period, that it has been vital to anyone working on Pope and some of his contemporaries. . . . . Take, for example, the Twickenham edition of Pope. We know that it would be a totally different thing if Dr. Griffith had never done the basic work on texts and editions on which the Twickenham volumes rest." This work, however, as Dr. Griffith projected it, was never completed. The finished bibliography would have included another volume, devoted to *Popiana,* the quarrel literature, a book which was well under way when ill health forced him to slow down his activities.

Dr. Griffith's service to scholarship was further extended by three other major activities. First, his vision and efforts brought to The University of Texas the Wrenn Library, the George A. Aitken Library, the Miriam Lutcher Stark Library, and subsequently other collections and individual pieces, to form the *Rare Book Collections,* which has now been expanded into the Humanities Research Center. He was also instrumental in the establishment of the University of Texas Press, in the selection of its director, Mr. Frank Wardlaw, and in the formulation of its policies. Finally, and certainly not least important, Dr. Griffith was responsible for the founding of the *Conference of College Teachers of English of Texas* and served as the president of the organization during its first five years. In 1933, when there were no regional branches of national organizations of college English teachers and, therefore, no meetings in Texas or nearby states to bring teachers together, Dr. Griffith invited English teachers from the widely separated colleges of Texas for a conference at The University of Texas, and at this meeting, under his direction, was formed the state organization which has met annually, except during two years of World War II, since 1933.

The twenty-fifth annual meeting of the *Conference* was dedicated to the honoring of Dr. Griffith, the founder. Plans were under the general direction of the 1959 and 1960 presidents, Joseph D. Thomas of The Rice University and E. Hudson Long of Baylor University, respectively, and of the secretary-treasurer, Truman W. Camp of Texas Technological College. The meeting was held on March 26, 1960, at the Shamrock-Hilton Hotel, in Houston, with The Rice University and the University of Houston as hosts. Of the several hundred college English teachers present, almost all had been directly or indirectly associated with Dr. Griffith.

The papers included in this volume, exclusive of the one by Dr. Griffith himself, were read at the Houston meeting. The address treating of the duties and responsibilities of the college teacher of English, a matter that had always been of deep concern to Dr. Griffith, was presented at a luncheon by Professor George W. Sherburn, a long-time friend and coworker in the eighteenth-century. The two papers concerned with Dr. Griffith himself and his contributions to education in Texas were read by his close friend and colleague Professor Robert A. Law, and by Dr. Fannie E. Ratchford, who, as librarian of the Wrenn Library and later of the entire Rare

Book Collections, worked directly with Dr. Griffith for almost forty years. The papers of Dr. Griffith's friend and fellow-scholar Professor Alan D. McKillop, The Rice University, and of his former student Professor Leonard N. Wright, Arkansas Agricultural and Mechanical College, treat phases of two subjects to which Dr. Griffith had given considerable attention—the "pattern" pieces in literature and the history of ideas—and illustrate the seminal nature of his scholarship.

To publish this volume The Humanities Research Center of The University of Texas and the University of Texas Press have joined with the *Conference of College Teachers of English of Texas.* The project has received enthusiastic support from Chancellor Harry H. Ransom, of The University of Texas; and the pleasure and the responsibility of seeing the book through the press have been shared by Professor Thomas P. Harrison and Mr. Frank Wardlaw of the University. It is hoped that Dr. Griffith, who bore the Torch, would approve.

MARY TOM OSBORNE

San Antonio College
San Antonio, Texas

GRIFFITH AS A TEXAS PIONEER

BEFORE WE EVER MET, Dr. Griffith and I possessed much in common. We were both natives of Carolina, born seventy-six miles and six years apart. A half-dozen years also separated our respective graduations from small denominational colleges in South Carolina only thirty miles distant, and each of us taught a year or two in college and in Carolina schools, then went north for graduate study. After he had imparted English four years to students at The University of Texas, I joined him there, and we were fellow laborers and intimate friends almost fifty years. Because of these common experiences I came to know him well and understand him better.

One of my earliest and most vivid recollections of him concerns his action at a faculty meeting in The University of Texas about 1909, when he was a newly made adjunct professor with vote, and I was a nonvoting instructor. The faculty, then numbering about fifty or sixty, used to meet in a comparatively small room centering about a large table that provided seats for a dozen or more members. At the head of this table sat President Mezes facing Judge Clark, the secretary, while senior professors of various departments occupied chairs flanking him on either side. All we lesser lights were accustomed to sit some distance away along the walls of the room. The resulting effect on faculty discussion is evident. Such was the established tradition, but this day there was a shocking change, apparent as I entered the room. Young Dr. Griffith had boldly taken a seat among the inner circle of Battle, Benedict, Garrison, Townes, and others. No written rule had been violated and no punishment was assessed. Soon afterward the faculty changed its meeting place to another room, where differences in rank were not so obvious. Yet Griffith's juvenile delinquency made on some of us a lasting impression. I mention the incident now neither to praise nor to blame him, but to illustrate his willingness occasionally to break with established tradition in a manner contrary to the habitual grace of an eighteenth-century English gentleman or an Oxford don. On such occasions he resembled not Dr. Morgan Callaway so much as the unpredictable J. Frank Dobie. That is, he had certain traits of a daring Texas pioneer.

The spirit of the pioneer again moved Griffith, still merely an adjunct professor in 1916, to propose an elaborate academic festival on the campus to honor Shakespeare at the tercentenary of his death. Appended to this celebration, unwisely, I think, were similar honors to William Harvey, who in 1616 announced his discovery of the circulation of the human blood. To arrange for the twin festival Griffith took the time-honored course of having a faculty committee appointed, of which naturally he was made chairman. He exercised more than a chairman's authority in almost every detail, and with the help of numerous friends, especially feminine, he saw to it that there should be a tremendous costumed pageant, dancing and parades by almost a thousand university students and Austin school children, public lectures on Shakespeare by Barrett Wendell of Harvard, John M. Manly of Chicago, and Judge R. L. Batts of Austin, and on Harvey by William Ritter of California. All these lectures were afterward published by the University in somewhat humble form together with a few other contributions honoring Shakespeare and Harvey. Now I must acknowledge that this academic festival was not the earliest recorded in Texas. In extent and grandeur it ranked as a mere satellite beside that launched four years earlier to mark the inaguration of Rice Institute. Austin is not Houston, nor ever has been, and Griffith was not blessed with the resources of President Lovett. But for most of those who saw it the show initiated by Griffith was something new and glorious, so that his own final word of description in the memorial volume is a characteristic understatement: "Our April days were a gala season, most successful and long to be remembered."

I trust I shall not invade the province of Dr. Fannie Ratchford, who is to follow me and who can tell so much better than anyone else the full story of Griffith's own collection of rare volumes about Alexander Pope and his contemporaries, and how this led to the Littlefield purchase of the Chicago Wrenn Library in 1918 as a gift to The University of Texas. Suffice it now to say that Griffith on learning that the Wrenn holdings were for sale "sauntered," as President Vinson put it, into the President's office and persuaded him to approach some possible donor who might provide $225,000 for such a worthy addition to institutional prestige. The entire plan was carried out, Major Littlefield donating the needed money. Many in this room can testify to the riches of the Wrenn Library and to the physical beauty of the place in which it has always been housed. Fitting ceremonies accompanied the opening of the collection, with Dr. Griffith making the chief address. Then President Vinson announced Griffith's appointment as Curator of the Wrenn Library, an unsalaried office demanding continued hard and expert labor for many years.

In designating this service as that of a Texas pioneer I am not unmindful of blessings to the state by not a few lovers of books whose valuable collections have eventually been brought to serve the public. Yet such a generous donation as that of Major Littlefield for the specific purchase of what some would term antiquated tomes was unprecedented in Texas at the time and unappreciated by some high officials of the University. Griffith was dreaming like Joseph of old and seeing visions of better days to come. It was two score years later that the Harvard Club of extra-$100,000 philanthropists came into being. One also recalls that the Hebrew boy's dreams were derided by his jealous brethren, who resented his prophecy that they would bow down to an upstart younger brother. What Griffith foresaw was the cultural maturity of the state he loved. So far as Texas is concerned, one wonders if certain recent generous donors to the libraries of Baylor, Rice, and Texas Christian universities would have done so well without the precedent of Major Littlefield to stir them on. Certainly the appropriation two years later by the Texas Legislature of $10,000 for the purchase of the Aitken Library would have been impossible.

Acquisition of the Wrenn and the Aitken libraries encouraged Griffith to complete his long-cherished plan of writing a bibliography of Pope, which the University published in two parts in 1922 and 1927. Although I believe I read in proof every line of the two books, I would not venture a personal appraisal of their value to eighteenth-century scholars. Fortunately Professor Sherburn and other specialists who have a right to be heard have expressed their judgment. From them I gather that the work at once became and will long remain the one standard authority on a most difficult topic in the history of English literature, a monument of patient and meticulous learning. In Europe and in America, Dr. Griffith has been repeatedly recognized as a great bibliographer. If any other Texan has approached his stature in the field, I know not his name.

The University of Texas organized its graduate faculty in 1925, and Griffith was one of its original members. Two years later, when our first candidate for the doctor of philosophy in English received that distinction, his dissertation was written under the supervision of Griffith. This candidate, the first English Ph.D. from any Texas institution, was Floyd Stovall, who just twenty years later became president of this Conference. He is today chairman of the English Department of the University of Virginia and one of the best-known scholars in American literature. His temporal primacy in winning this degree was perhaps accidental, as was also Griffith's primacy in training him, for he was soon followed by many other candidates who chose various masters. The historical fact, however, is that Griffith's pupil won pioneer honors, and in succeeding years almost a score of men and women received the same degree under his supervision. Their common loyalty and personal gratitude to their preceptor will probably be touched on by another speaker.

All this pioneer work led to the event that underlies the present program, the first meeting in 1933 of the Texas Conference of College Teachers of English. Its beginning was quite modest. Griffith wrote letters to a number of college teachers of his acquaintance, inviting them to come to Austin and possibly set up a new organization. As usual, he personally supervised the operational problems without much bother over a constitution. I know that he appointed himself to preside and Dr. E. G. Fletcher to act as secretary, and that without previous notice called on me at the dining table to make an address of welcome. At the time I was carrying my fractured left arm in a conspicuous sling, and the only recollection that I now have of what I said is that the bird with the broken pinion never soared so high again. The governing idea, however, that Texas college teachers of English should gather once a year to discuss their own problems, took hold of those present and quickly spread. For four years thereafter Griffith served as president of the new organization and three more meetings were held in Austin. Then at his suggestion a new president was selected, and the 1938 meeting took place on the Southern Methodist campus in Dallas. Thus our founding father cut loose the strings restraining his infant, who has waxed stronger and stronger ever since.

Griffith's last community service that I shall mention, and one of the most far-reaching, came in connection with the establishment of the University of Texas Press. True, in this case he was not the earliest Texas pioneer, for the Southern Methodist Press at Dallas was well on its feet and had sponsored many worthy volumes before The University of Texas ventured to follow. Yet Griffith envisaged long before it came into being the creation of a press worthy of the institution whose name it would bear. To provide this, he believed, would enlarge the bounds of human knowledge with publications of other than commercial value, placing "emphasis on scholarly studies in many fields and Southwest regional material." On his appointment by President Painter as chairman of a committee to investigate the project, he collected facts about other presses, brought to Austin experts for consultation, laid out plans, and finally secured action from the Board of Regents. In 1950 the University of Texas Press was established, the committee headed by him chose the present director, and in recognition of what he did a large and striking portrait of Griffith hangs today in the headquarters of the Press.

I could ramble on much longer in this reminiscent vein, which may not accord with the chairman's purpose in asking me to participate. The temptation to garrulity looms large when one of my age is permitted to talk of the vagaries of a familiar friend. To guard against this I have attempted to confine myself to one facet of his personality: his willingness to see Texas beyond the age of cowboys, even of millionaire oil men, and to follow his vision at a time when this vision was not shared by his scornful fellows.

If Dr. Griffith, sitting in the obscure corner of heaven that he once said he hoped to occupy, is looking down on this spot, I believe he will be pleased with what we are doing. For during his long life he had fewer monuments erected to him, less compensation for what he was trying to do than he really deserved. True, Furman University, his original alma mater, gave him an honorary degree, this Conference and the South-Central Modern Language Association, each, elected him as the first one of its honorary members. Yet he lost an only son, his first-born, in infancy, and was deprived most of his lifetime of the home that he really desired. Three times that I know of, circumstances or deliberate action deprived him of a certain distinction that he seemed to have earned. The ill-starred *Memorial Volume to Shakespeare and Harvey,* Griffith's brain child, was dedicated at Griffith's suggestion to Morgan Callaway, Jr., and contains his own name only in the Appendix and then rather casually. The 1944 volume of *Texas Studies in English* received a special appropriation from the Board of Regents of the University as an eighteenth-century number, to which Griffith, himself, contributed the leading article on "Pope Editing Pope." In addition to the usual contributions from the Texas faculty, this volume contains notable studies by George Sherburn, Arthur E. Case, and Louis A.

Landa. Now my understanding at the time was that the Regential appropriation was intended as recognition of Griffith's labors not too long before his retirement, but the book is not dedicated to him nor is there any indication of honors due. What proved a more serious disappointment than these two possible accidents was the silent removal of his title as Curator of the Wrenn Library after many years of service, when another Pharaoh arose who knew not Joseph.

In view of these facts, I am tempted to reveal what few of you have probably learned about certain plans in connection with the magnificent academic center about to be erected on the campus of the University. This building along with its extensive open shelves for popular undergraduate reading is to have, on one of its upper floors, several studies for graduate research in particular periods. The Board of Regents has already voted that the study devoted to the Eighteenth Century will bear the name of Reginald Harvey Griffith.

Coming back once more to the subject of Texas pioneers, I owe to Barker's *Life of Stephen F. Austin,* the scholarly father of Texas, a striking anecdote of his death. Says Barker: "He waked from a dream thinking that the United States had recognized its [Texas'] independence, and died happy in that belief. His last words were, 'Texas recognized. Archer told me so. Did you see it in the papers?' " Griffith's lonely last years were brightened by unceasing kindness from many of those he had trained, and by the realization that some of his midsummer-night dreams had taken substance, his airy nothings had been given a local habitation and a name. More will follow.

ROBERT ADGER LAW

GRIFFITH AND RARE BOOKS

I

THE OPENING OF THE Wrenn Library at The University of Texas early in 1919, the gift of Major George W. Littlefield, touched off a chain reaction which, within a period of forty years, raised an unknown college library to a notable research center.

Other acquisitions followed in spectacular succession: the George A. Aitken, the Miriam Lutcher Stark, and the E. L. DeGolyer libraries, with many important smaller collections and single volumes, all contributing to the fulfillment of Sir Swante Palm's earlier prophetic bequest.

The *deus ex machina* in this amazing trend of events, the hero of a fabulous story with fantastic incidents worthy of endless detective novels, was Dr. Reginald Harvey Griffith of the University's English Faculty, whose name is synonymous with Rare Book Collections at The University of Texas. His was the guiding counsel that established the gifts as a vital force in the culture of the state and a cynosure of the book world.

Back of Dr. Griffith and, no doubt, inspiring him was the dream of Sir Swante Palm, a Swedish immigrant who landed in Galveston in 1844, Texas' first conscious and purposeful book collector. In course of a long life he amassed about ten thousand volumes, much manuscript, and many documents looking backward to the culture of the Old World and forward to the rich, proud Texas he saw in the making. Near the end of his life, in 1897, he presented this library to the infant state university at Austin, and with it offered himself as director, "to teach the young men and women of Texas how best to use these great books of all time." He died within two years of making the gift, before The University of Texas had caught his vision.

The torch lay as it had fallen from his hand, when a few years later, in the autumn of 1904, Dr. Griffith returned from his summer vacation, bringing in his baggage a small group of books which he had diligently hunted out in English bookshops. Among the Griffith papers at The University of Texas there is an interesting account of these purchases:

My interest in bookcollecting was accidental in origin, and gradually but—alack-a-day!—geometrically progressive in its growth. The summer after I began teaching the poetry of Dryden and Pope I bought an odd volume of Pope's *Works,* containing the "Dunciad" and a list of early editions of that virulent satire. The latter attracted my attention, and remained in memory. The next summer I spent in London, mainly at work in The British Museum, but I found time for many an expedition among bookstores. . . . I secured a number of old books and pamphlets concerning Dryden and his contemporaries, and some on Pope, two or three early editions of the "Dunciad" among other things. The insiduous dealers graciously volunteered to send me their catalogues free. I acquiesced readily. Poor bird, I saw no lime.

This record omits a climactic ancedote which he told somewhat wryly, many years later, at a dinner given him by a group of his graduate students on his eightieth birthday. As he neared the end of this first visit to England, with his return passage paid and arrangements made for money to meet him in New York, he determined to spend all his remaining cash in hand on books. As a result of the orgy, somewhat more abandoned than he had planned, he reached his New York hotel with only the fraction of a dollar in his pocket. Unperturbed, he wired a sister in Washington, according to previous arrangement, but reckoned without weekend irregularities in communication. The sister was out of town and did not get his wire until Monday. In the meantime her brother in New York, forgetting that meals might be charged to his hotel room, went hungry.

In due course, the promised book catalogues began to come in. Dr. Griffith continues the story:

By accident again, I acquired several more editions of the *Dunciad*. Curiosity now became keen. How many of these early editions were there? To this day, no man knows positively through how many editions the poem passed before it was twenty-three years old. I determined to collect every one of them, a thing which has never been done in the world yet. I am still determined and I am still trying. At the present time I could describe the distinguishing peculiarity of fifty-three such editions, using the word "edition" loosely. I have forty-three out of the possible fifty-three.

In 1912, when Dr. Griffith again sailed for Europe, this time for a sabbatical year, the prime object of his trip "so far as book collecting played a part," was to add to his set of *Dunciads*. He had forty when he left home, and was able, after the most strenuous search, to add only three new varieties.

Extending his interest, he found good hunting, however, for pamphlets subsidiary to the *Dunciad* making up the "War of the Dunces." "How many . . . there are," he states, "it is impossible to say. The guesser must proceed even more vaguely than in estimating the number of editions of the *Dunciad*. My guess, a rash one, is that there are about three hundred and fifty of them. I shall never own all these, but I want every one of them."

In London Bertram Dobell remained, as of old, his adviser and helper, but Dr. Griffith himself roamed wide in his quest. In the afternoons, after the British Museum closed, and on holidays he raked London for the books he wanted, wandering in "little old unlisted shops in lanes, alleys, mews and markets." Sometimes he rode far out on one of the city's fifty-two bus lines, noting bookshops along the way to visit as he walked back.

Remembering a bookdealer in Leyton, from whose catalogue he had several times secured bargains, he wasted two hours in seeking him out, only to find that no books were sold on the place. His was strictly a catalogue business. However, though Dr. Griffith obtained no book from this man, he gratefully records, "I acquired a piece of information from which I derived many happy hours. He was the first to tell me of the stalls in Farringdon Road." There is pure joy in Dr. Griffith's description of frequent walks from the British Museum to Farringdon Road where specimens of every variety of books were to be found at prices ranging from two to fifty cents. Besides the fun of beating the dealer down, there was always the chance of making a sensational find. The best Dr. Griffith ever did, however, was to buy for one penny a book which had once belonged to R. B. Haydon, whom he knew as a painter under the sobriquet "The Cockney Raphael," an intimate of Wordsworth and Coleridge.

In November, to escape London's fogs, Dr. Griffith fled to the continent, where he continued his book hunting.

Paris and Berlin were a keen disappointment, for in either city English books were few and expensive, but Switzerland was more productive. In Basel he "picked up two or three good things," and Lausanne gave him the earliest translation of Pope's works into French, with valuable notes, and an American volume containing an excellent critical essay on Edgar Allan Poe, which he purchased for six cents as a present for his friend Dr. Killis Campbell. But the book Dr. Griffith particularly wanted to buy in Lausanne was not forthcoming, a criticism of Pope's *Essay on Man* by Professor Crousaz of the Faculty of Philosophy of The University of Lausanne. The book is in Dr. Griffith's library, but it came later by another route.

Back in England in the spring, Dr. Griffith took a disappointing and disillusioning fling in the auction rooms, coming out, however, with one gratifying bargain. At a certain sale he instructed a bookdealer to bid as high as forty shillings for a group of folio poems by Pope bound together in one volume. The dealer replied that he would himself pay as high as sixty shillings for the pieces to go into stock. By good luck, the sale fell upon a day when the President of France was paying a state visit to London. Few bidders appeared in the auction room, and by a fluke the volume was knocked down for sixteen shillings. The dealer, however, required Dr. Griffith to pay twenty-five shillings for the prize. "But, nevertheless," gloated he, "I got my book for a third of what it was worth—thanks to M. Poincaré, President of the French Republic."

Combining book hunting with sight-seeing, he visited many a bookshop in "the provinces." In Cambridge, at a booth in a marketplace, he found "excellent picking." "One little book," he says, "is interesting for two reasons—it has on its title-page a rough portrait of Pope that is almost a caricature. The publisher, who was the famous 'pirate-printer,' Curll, says he had his sign painter do the original. And over the authorship of the story, which is named *Prince Ti-Ti,* Macaulay got into a controversy."

I do not know at what point the plan for a bibliography of Pope took definite form in Dr. Griffith's mind, but his library gives evidence that the thought shaped his collecting for years. The over-all pattern he followed is indicated in the introductions to the two volumes of the *Bibliography,* 1922–1927. For the work he had in mind, he said, he must examine and rightly place in date and circumstance Pope's every extant writing and saying. But Pope's writings had not been fully identified and catalogued, and "collecting must precede cataloguing."

He must, he said, make himself familiar with 1) general bibliographies such as those by Lowndes and Allibone, with the catalogues of the Dyce, Hoe, Lefferts, and Chew Collections, and with catalogues of such sales as the Solly, Grant, and Prideaux libraries; 2) the work of preceding scholars—Croker, Thoms, Dilke, and Carruthers in the mid-nineteenth century—and the current researches of his contemporaries: Professors Arthur Ellicott Case and George Wiley Sherburn, who had recently extended the Pope canon; 3) every scrap of Pope's works signed and unsigned, including his letters, even to newspapers containing advertisements he composed and quotations from his works, and all books attributed to him; 4) miscellanies; 5) all sources of information regarding Pope's publishers and printers: Tonson, Lewis, Lintot, Motte, Bettenham, John Wright, the Widow Dodd, Wilford, Curll, Thomas Cooper, Gilliver, Dodsley, the Knaptons, and Henry Woodfall, names which account for many volumes in the Griffith Library; 6) books such as *Agreable Variety: Art of English Poetry,* and *Complete Art of English Poetry,* containing quotations from Pope; 7) three important eighteenth-century magazines carrying lists of newly published books: Wilford's *Monthly Chronicle,* Cave's *Gentleman's Magazine,* and *Grub-*

street Journal; and 8) allusion books as an indication of his popularity.

In this outline Dr. Griffith equated the term "collecting" with seeing, examining, and describing, rather than personally acquiring, though all the time that he was thus "collecting" in public and private libraries, he was acquiring items for himself as rapidly as the market and his financial means gave opportunity.

II

AN IMPORTANT Pope collection in America, which Dr. Griffith knew he must see, was that included in the library of John Henry Wrenn, which, since the collector's death in 1911, had remained intact in the family home in Chicago. In response to permission granted him by the executors of the Wrenn estate, he visited this library at Christmastime in 1917, and from that inspection brought back to President R. E. Vinson of The University of Texas information of its fabulous riches—5200 titles in English and American literature, all first or early editions, from Edmund Spenser to the year of Mr. Wrenn's death. This information, laid before Major George W. Littlefield, Chairman of the Board of Regents of The University of Texas, persuaded him to present the Wrenn Library to the University, together with a special room to house it, planned and executed by Thomas Tallmadge. Colonel George W. Brackenridge, another member of the Board of Regents, asked and received permission to donate the handsome five-volume catalogue of the Wrenn library, printed by Chiswick Press.

This catalogue (one hundred copies) distributed as gifts among research centers, projected the usefulness of the Wrenn Library around the world, and greatly enhanced the prestige of The University of Texas.

The importance of Major Littlefield's gift and Dr. Griffith's wise and generous organization of it as curator can hardly be exaggerated as landmarks in the advancement of The University of Texas toward the designation of its founders as a school of the first class. If the acquisition of this library did not actually initiate the present graduate school, it drew to a focus the ambitions and forces already working within the several faculties toward that end, and it brought into envious world notice an institution whose very name and location were previously unknown beyond its own region.

Within two years of the opening of the Wrenn Library, Dr. Griffith, enlisting the help of State Senator Louis H. Darwin, secured for the University another closely related group of books of like nature and importance, and somewhat larger in number of volumes. This was the library of the renowned scholar George A. Aitken of London, the laboratory, so to speak, out of which came his forty or more standard reference works pertaining to seventeenth- and eighteenth-century English literature. Its range and riches are suggested in the reminder that it brought to Texas all the variants of all the Chaucer folios from 1526 to 1602 and laid the foundations of Texas' present well-known collection of seventeenth- and eighteenth-century English newspapers. The two libraries dovetailed perfectly and, housed near together, each doubled the other's value.

The publicity attending the coming to Texas of the Wrenn and Aitken libraries brought to light an astonishing accumulation of books and manuscripts in Orange, Texas, gathered by Mrs. Miriam Lutcher Stark in her own home and for her own pleasure.

Though Mrs. Stark had long been closely connected with the University—her husband had served on its Board of Regents, and her son was even then chairman of the Board—no one on the campus knew of the existence of this startling library. Public interest in the discovery made it well-nigh inevitable that the Miriam Lutcher Stark Library would join the Wrenn and Aitken as a third in Rare Book Collections at The University of Texas.

As early as April, 1924, Mrs. Stark allowed Dr. Griffith to draw freely upon her books for a notable—to Byron enthusiasts, a sensational—Byron Centennial Exhibition described in a catalogue compiled by Dr. Griffith and Howard Mumford Jones. The presentation of the Library was made in 1926, and selected books were brought up from time to time as needed. The library as a whole, however, was not transferred until a suitable suite of rooms on the Rare Book Floor of the New Library Building was ready to receive it.

Following their collector's personal taste in reading, the Stark shelves are rich beyond measure in the Elizabethans, in the Romantics, and in Victorian poets and novelists. Mediaeval illuminated manuscripts; the four Shakespeare folios, together with Shakespearian source books; Sidney's *Arcadia;* all the Dickens and Thackeray novels in original parts, with many thousand literary manuscripts and historical documents, fill numerous gaps in the other collections. The Stark Byron group alone is beyond evaluation, ranking, both in first editions and manuscripts, second only to that of Sir John Murray, III, of London, grandson of Byron's publisher.

The range of the Rare Book Collections was further extended in 1946, when Mr. E. L. DeGolyer of Dallas, a well-known collector of materials relating to the American Southwest, presented to the University a group of 1200 volumes laying the foundation for a broad and strong library of modern English and American literature. Though several authors, Walt Whitman and Samuel Butler, for instance, approach completeness, others, including H. G. Wells, Hardy, and Galsworthy, are represented only by their hardest-to-procure pieces. Mr. DeGolyer explained that at the time he was exploring modern writers his Southwest Collection left him little shelf room for this passing interest. He bought, therefore, as the chance offered, only those pieces known to exist in few copies, leaving to the convenient future the comparatively easy task of adding the more common items.

Too numerous to describe or even to list here, are many one-subject and one-author gifts and purchases that further enriched Rare Book Collections under Dr. Griffith's wise and discriminating oversight, such as a remarkably rich collection of W. B. Yeats and the Gino Speranza-Arthur Livingston collection of Italo-American cultural relations.

The last notable group which Dr. Griffith saw added was his own library, which he was wont to describe with formula-like brevity as about four thousand volumes centering around Pope and Dryden. But this is hardly a fair statement, for it tends to obscure notable holdings of Swift, Addison, Steele, Arbuthnot, Cibber, and a score of other greater or lesser eighteenth-century writers impossible to duplicate in today's market; it omits volumes of scarce and important newspapers; and it ignores enviable groups of Milton, Byron, and the Victorian poets.

By the standard of the Wrenn and Stark shelves, Dr. Griffith's books have little of the comeliness that an interior decorator would desire. Scrupulously kept as bought, a good many are without binding; most are in old calf or sheep, some with hinges broken and covers tied on. But bibliographers and scholars value their condition. All are known as "good copies," while some are large paper, and others are uncut. With the wisdom and integrity of a true bibliographer, he resisted all persuasion to have his volumes rebound, lest a vestige of their personality be lost. Tight binding interfered with his probings among their leaves to learn how they were put together. More warmly still, he insisted upon keeping his thin folios and broadsides unbound between stiff boards, the better to examine them in their entirety. The nicety of his fingers in handling his books matched the skill of his eyes in reading their make-up.

With the opening of the Tower of the present Main Building as offices for the English Faculty, Dr. Griffith brought his books from his home to a room—dubbed, naturally enough, "The Grotto"—adjoining his office, that they might the more conveniently supplement Rare Book Collections. Through the last twenty years of his life he was plied with inquiries from dealers, scholars, and institutions concerning the intended disposal of his library. To all he answered, "I have always hoped that my books would stay at The University of Texas." The University, negotiating with his daughters, made the purchase a few months before he died.

III

A COLLEAGUE OF Dr. Griffith in his earlier years on the campus remarked to him, "I verily believe that if someone gave you a half-million dollars you would spend it all on books." But Dr. Griffith's passion for books was no distorting oddity of nature or taste. It was rather the logical expression of his finely balanced and remarkably disciplined mind. Books, he reasoned, represent the accumulated thought and knowledge of the ages. As a scholar he must, so far as possible, make their wisdom his own, and as a teacher he must train young men and women, even as Sir Swante Palm had dreamed, how to expand their legacy for future generations.

In assembling a great library at The University of Texas he followed the principles he had used in building his own. He would make Rare Book Collections serviceable rather than spectacular; selective rather than cumulative; and scholarly rather than popular. As in pre-Wrenn Library days, when he used his own books to introduce students to the techniques of research bibliography, he now endeavored through exhibitions, group talks, and personal chats "to bring them acquainted with" the wealth at their command. Always he insisted that it was not the number of books alone that counted, but the individual importance of each book and its relation to the group. When negotiating for the Aitken Collection, his strongest plea for the purchase money was, "We are not asking for seven thousand additional books, valuable though they are individually; we are asking for *these* books, assembled by a great scholar and representing his knowledge and discrimination."

Dr. Griffith's own knowledge of English printed books was phenomenal. Even in his last years, when his working hours were shortening, he did not cease to read the innumerable catalogues that came to his desk, passing judgment on each item listed not already on Rare Book shelves, as to its claim on the small purchasing fund at his disposal. And through this same period, when temptation was strong to multiply numbers and splash in shallow pools of popular book collecting, he maintained the unity of Rare Book Collections on the high level he had set.

IV

IN THE COURSE of its first thirty-five years of life, i.e., from its opening in 1883 to the coming of the Wrenn Library, The University of Texas conferred approximately forty Master's degrees in English, all directed by Professor Morgan Callaway, Jr., except three which fell to the lot of Dr. James Finch Royster. Within the following seven years, the number leaped to approximately seventy, directed by a proportionally enlarged staff. Dr. Griffith's share was nineteen theses, not counting half a dozen more which he directed jointly with a colleague.

Though a fair proportion of this increased interest in the Master's degree is to be accounted for by growth in the student body following World War I, one cannot fail to read in it the tremendous impact of enlarged library facilities. And here it should be remembered that the Department of History, inspired by Dr. Griffith's example and led by Dr. Charles W. Hackett, had in 1921 seized the opportunity to acquire, in Mexico, the unequalled private library of Genaro García, a purchase which started rolling a Texas snowball of research material in Latin-American history and culture which continues to gather size and force.

But the M.A. degree could not for long contain the growing intellectual demands of University of Texas students. It is a fitting tribute to Dr. Griffith's services that the first Ph.D. degree in the English Department—conferred upon Floyd Herman Stovall, in 1927—was directed by him and that Mr. Stovall's oral examination was held in the Wrenn Room.

The most fruitful, perhaps, of all Dr. Griffith's efforts to train scholars in the use of libraries was his course in eighteenth-century studies, which he offered each term, including most summers, for more than twenty years, never repeating the subject or problem studied. It is doubtful that the English Department ever offered a more stimulating exercise in scholarly exploration or better training in research methods than this seminar. By its nature it attracted able and ambitious students, most of whom were potential Ph.D. candidates. But Dr. Griffith never took advantage of it to hold good students to himself. On the contrary, using his judgment as to the need of the individual, he pointed many to his colleagues on the campus. Others whose circumstances permitted, he advised to seek out the graduate schools best suited to their needs in library and faculty. If need were, he helped them secure fellowships to that end.

One of the fledglings thus pushed out of the Texas nest was Professor Louis Landa, now of Princeton University, whose many letters, found in Dr. Griffith's desk, acknowledge how great was his debt to him through the years. A similar series written by James Lee Cate, Professor of History at the University of Chicago, shows that Dr. Griffith's interest in young scholars was no respecter of their subject of study. Indeed he seemed always to carry in mind, along with his own problems, those of his fellow teachers in sciences as well as in the humanities. In casual meetings or in notes he habitually passed on to them relevant information he had come upon in his wide ranging through books.

The profound respect in which Dr. Griffith was held by leading scholars the world over after the 1922 publication of his *Alexander Pope: A Bibliography,* is not fully realized however, by even his closest colleague, until he scans the thousands of letters making up Dr. Griffith's scholarly correspondence. The reader of these letters will be amazed to find how many of the now familiar literary discoveries announced within the past twenty-five years, projects undertaken and completed, problems solved, and judgments pronounced, were first submitted to Dr. Griffith for testing. Rarely did his knowledge fall short, and never, except for T. J. Wise's tirade concerning the First Edition of Pope's *Essay on Man,* was his judgment challenged.

Dr. Griffith's success in building a great research library at

The University of Texas is the more remarkable in that it was done without administrative authority. Except for the short-lived honorary title "Curator of the Wrenn Library," he was never *officially* connected with Rare Book Collections. But thanks to his wide knowledge of the book world and consistent use of a faculty member's privilege to address recommendations and requests to the President, the department was never without his wise counsel and leadership. So close was his connection that, across the campus and throughout the state, Rare Book Collections was commonly known as "Dr. Griffith's child." And to him came the happiest of a parent's rewards: he saw his child grow to man's stature in his own image, serving scholarship, even as he had planned.

FANNIE E. RATCHFORD

CHRISTIAN MORTALISM: A PROSPECTUS FOR THE HISTORY OF AN IDEA

THOSE WHO HAVE HAD the privilege of sitting through any of Professor R. H. Griffith's seminars on Pope or Dryden will recall that one of his major interests was the history of ideas. The generation of Griffith disciples to which I belonged—the 1930's—will remember especially his repeated reference to Professor Bury's *The Idea of Progress* as the model for such studies. At that time also Vernon Parrington's *Main Currents in American Thought* was beginning to have an impact on American scholarship and was accorded an occasional mention in his lectures; or his well-known flair for philosophy might prompt him to a citation from A. N. Whitehead's *Adventures of Ideas,* then just off the press. It is gratifying to note that the spate of books on ideas which have been printed since that decade soundly confirms Dr. Griffith's belief that the history of ideas was a field worthy of a scholar's efforts.

In such an aura it is not surprising that a number of his graduate students should devote all or a part of their research to tracing the growth and development of ideas or movements. Examination of the titles of the doctoral dissertations written under his guidance will reveal that a goodly percentage were ideological studies, and I am pleased to include my own dissertation under that category.

If a canvass of Dr. Griffith's protégés were to be made to determine how best to "characterize" him, I am sure the unanimous choice would be the phrase from his beloved Pope, "guide, philosopher, and friend." All of us were deeply indebted to him for the many suggestions as to source material which he furnished us from his great store of information; and his kindly patience and friendly encouragement helped us surmount many of the difficulties which beset us on the rugged road to the doctorate. In my own case I know that his fine sense of style and his keen critical sense contributed greatly to the improvement of my somewhat labored sentences.

As I think back on my association with Dr. Griffith, I have a feeling that he would have preferred us to eliminate the praise and accent the scholarship. It is with this feeling that I offer this paper, based in part on research done under his supervision, as a tribute to his memory.

Dr. Griffith was aware of a study that I had previously made of Milton's belief in the mortality of the soul, and when the time came for me to choose a topic for the doctoral dissertation, I was delighted when he suggested that I pursue the idea further. I am sure that he knew what a large topic I had undertaken, since he also suggested that for purposes of thoroughness I had better stay within a convenient time limit, which by a not too strange coincidence happened to be within his own field of *expertise.* Since completing the dissertation I have worked independently on the topic and am now in a position to give something like a complete history of the idea of mortalism from its beginnings in the early stages of Christianity up to the present. This paper represents a prospectus of that history.

Mortalism may be defined as the belief that the soul either is to be identified with the life of the body, or, if it is a separable substance, is incapable of conscious survival after death. This idea is much older than Christianity. There is strong evidence that the Hebrews believed that the soul was mortal, and it is also a well-known fact that the Greek atomists held that the soul-stuff was dissipated at death and ceased to function as an individual being.

A number of the early Church Fathers took the position that the soul was naturally mortal, but that it received immortality through divine grace—a point of view widely adopted by later mortalists. The first true mortalists on record were a religious sect that sprang up in Arabia in the third century A.D. They believed that the soul perished with the body but that it would be renewed at the resurrection. The heresy was short-lived, largely as the result of the friendly persuasion of Origen. Since several of the early Church Fathers describe this heresy, there is some possibility that it was more than a localized belief.

Church history does not mention the heresy again until the thirteenth century. Pope John XXII, who died in 1304, at one time openly accepted and advocated mortalism, but later recanted. The belief must have had considerable currency for several centuries thereabouts, for it was condemned by the Church councils in 1274, 1438, 1439, 1545, and 1563. During the Reformation the belief was embraced by certain of the Arminians and Socinians, and in particular by some of the Anabaptists. The latter, according to John Calvin, promulgated the doctrine both by preaching and by printed tracts. I was unable to locate any of these tracts, but fortunately Calvin's own tract on psychopannychism was available in several languages. It first appeared in Latin in 1542, was translated into French in 1548, and into English in 1581.

This is a very valuable document in the history of mortalism, because it gives a very thorough analysis of the arguments for and against the mortality of the soul. At this time the argument was confined mainly to Scriptural texts, and Calvin cites all the texts which the mortalists used to support their doctrine. For this reason, his tract probably contributed more to the spread of mortalism than to its suppression.

With the seventeenth century the scene shifts to England, where the first available book on mortalism written by a mortalist was published in 1644. Titled *Mans Mortalitie,* this book was written by a revolutionary named Richard Overton and was published in Amsterdam for distribution in England.

Overton uses the Bible more extensively than did the Anabaptists of Calvin's day, largely through the inclusion of some telling passages from the New Testament, I Corinthians, Chapter 15, for instance. He also cites authorities and uses rational arguments to support his beliefs on the soul. Aristotle, Lucretius, and Ambrose Paré, the latter a French physician of the preceding century, are his chief sources. Paré, in particular, furnished him with the evidence to show that the soul cannot function properly when the brain is injured, and he argued from this fact that the soul could not exist apart from the brain. He defines the soul as simply the higher functioning of the body. He also uses the psychology of animals to support his thesis that the soul does not exist apart from the body.

Except to the historian of mortalism, Overton is a relatively obscure figure. But two of his contemporary mortalists were well-known in the annals of the era. They are Thomas Hobbes, the philosopher, and John Milton, the poet.

Hobbes, whose views on the soul were first set forth in the *Leviathan* (1651), was such a thoroughgoing materialist that he denied incorporeity even to God. It is not surprising, then, that he did not believe in a separable soul, defining it as simply the "body alive." He contended that the soul of man became mortal when Adam failed to eat of the Tree of Life before partaking of the fruit of the Tree of Knowledge. Therefore the whole man now dies, but receives immortality at the resurrection through the grace of God.

Milton's unorthodox views on the soul did not come to light until the publication of his long-lost *Christian Doctrine* in 1825, although they might well have been suspected from certain passages in *Paradise Lost* and *Samson Agonistes.* He follows the usual route in providing the mortality of the soul: he argues from Scriptural texts, he cites both patristic and pagan authorities, he appeals to reason, and he answers objections. Being well versed in patristic literature and pagan philosophy, he uses these sources very effectively.

If we discount the Arabici back in the third century A.D., we may say that the 1650's produced the first distinct sect to believe in the mortality of the soul. (The Anabaptists were divided on the doctrine.) These were the Muggletonians, founded in 1652 by two cousins, John Reeve and Ludowick Muggleton. Both claimed to have had revelations directly from heaven designating them as the "witnesses" mentioned in Revelations (II, 3), and endowing them with the power to damn all who did not accept them as the "two prophets." The best statement of their doctrines can be found in *Joyful News from Heaven,* printed in 1658. They believed that the "soul dieth in the body," since it is only the life of the body. As is customary with those who receive revelations directly from heaven, they used no proof for any of their doctrines.

At the heart of the next cluster of mortalists was John Locke, another great philosopher. In the *Essay Concerning Human Understanding* (1690), Locke devotes considerable space to proving that the soul cannot think apart from the body, nor does he believe that the soul can have a conscious identity without memory, which in turn depends on the proper functioning of the brain. He is agnostic on the question of whether the soul is material or immaterial, but the bulk of his argument favors the possibility of a thinking material substance.

The clearest statement of his mortalistic beliefs occurs in *The Reasonableness of Christianity* (1695). Therein we note the familiar argument that Adam lost his immortality when he committed the original sin, and that, because of Adam, "all men are mortal." Death he defines as "nothing but a ceasing to be, the losing of all actions of life and sense."

When Richard Bentley attacked Locke for his views on the soul in the Boyle Lecture, "Matter and Motion Cannot Think," three of Locke's disciples came to his defense and thereby added considerably to the mass of mortalist literature. Henry Layton wrote more than a dozen pamphlets in defense of mortalism, concentrating his arguments mainly around the contention that the soul is a material thinking substance derived from the air we breathe and the food we eat. Like Overton, he refused to accept the Bible as the "very word of God," and boldly noted that the Four Gospels often have different accounts of the same story—the thieves at the Crucifixion, for instance.

Dr. William Coward, the second of Locke's defenders, shares with Muggleton, among the mortalists, the dubious distinction of having been called to public account for his unorthodoxy. His book, *Second Thoughts Concerning Human Soul* (1702), was burned by the common hangman on orders of the House of Commons.

Second Thoughts is one of the better books on mortalism, being thorough and well organized. He begins with a brief history of the concept of an immaterial soul, states what he considers the correct doctrine to be, and devotes three chapters to proving the mortality of the soul from Scriptural, rational, and philosophical points of view. He has an excellent bibliography, one that proved quite valuable to me in my research.

Anthony Collins, "the father of free thought," was the third disciple of Locke to enter into the controversy. He argued in a series of four letters addressed to Henry Dodwell and Samuel Clarke that it is within the power of God to confer the ability to think on a material substance. He defined the soul as the sum of the powers of the body and argued that these powers were destroyed at death. Thinking is a purely physical matter and will be resumed only with the renewal of the body at the resurrection.

Three churchmen make up the next group of mortalists. At the center was Joseph Priestley, Unitarian minister, scientist, and philosopher. Defending him and each other were two Anglican divines, Bishop Edmund Law and Archdeacon Francis Blackburne. Law seems to have been more of a "soul sleeper" than a true mortalist, taking the position that the "middle state" of souls after death was one of complete unconsciousness. Canon Blackburne, on the other hand, argued that there was no middle state and that the soul died with the body.

Priestley's views on the soul are contained in his *Disquisitions Relating to Soul and Matter* (1777). While the burden of his argument concerns the materiality of the soul, he does not neglect the stock proofs for its mortality. As a matter of fact we find a more thorough search of the Scriptures than in any preceding mortalist. Priestley defines thinking as an arrangement of the particles of the brain. Death disarranges these particles without destroying them, and at the resurrection they are rearranged in such wise as to make thinking possible again.

As we move over into the nineteenth century we note that there is a tendency for the belief in mortalism to decline in status but to increase in the number of adherents. The latter tendency, best described as "explosive," can be explained by the fact that three religious sects founded in that century all subscribed to the belief in the mortality of the soul. These were the so-called Seventh Day Adventists, the Christadelphians, and the International Bible Students Association, more commonly known as Jehovah's Witnesses.

The Adventists have splintered several times since their founding, and one of the causes was a difference of belief as to what happened to the soul at death. But the core group believes that the soul "sleeps" in the interval between death and the resurrection.

The Christadelphians, a much smaller sect, were founded in 1848 by Dr. John Thomas, shortly after coming to America from England. They believe that the soul of man is the same as that of an animal and dies along with the body. In many respects their doctrines resemble those of Priestley, but I suspect that both they and the Jehovah's Witnesses owe a great deal to the Muggletonians.

The Witnesses now number about 3,000,000 adherents all over the world. Founded by Charles Taze Russell in 1883, the sect has shown an amazing capacity for growth, especially in the last three decades. They are millenialists, and believe that we are already in the last thousand years. The first resurrection is slated for 1974, and will bring to life those who have just died. These in turn will prepare the way for preceding generations of the dead, and the process will continue in this reverse order until it reaches Adam and Eve. Their views on the soul and death are thoroughly mortalistic. Being fundamentalists, they restrict their arguments to the well-known Scriptural texts supporting the mortality of the soul.

This, then, is a somewhat sketchy overview of the history of the idea of mortalism from its inception to the present. Mortalism, after a weak start and a very slow early growth, is now in its most flourishing state. It is true that it does not now number among its adherents men of such caliber as Hobbes, Milton, Locke, or Priestley. But we must admit that in the struggle for existence which goes on in the world of ideas, as well as in the animal and the vegetable world, the belief in the soul's mortality has shown a capacity for survival surpassing many other Christian doctrines. And, if I may venture to prophesy, it has many more years yet to go before "wholly dying."

LEONARD N. WRIGHT

GRIFFITH'S PIONEER STUDY OF THE PROGRESS PIECE

IN THE BIBLIOGRAPHY of the recent Oxford volume, *English Literature in the Early Eighteenth Century: 1700–1740,* Bonamy Dobrée lists under studies in literary types Professor Griffith's article, "The Progress Piece of the Eighteenth Century" (*Texas Review,* V [1920], 218–233). I wish to go behind this entry and to discuss the article as an example of a productive scholar's work. Modest though the essay is, it represents the kind of work which makes a difference to other scholars and is likely to alter received patterns and to deepen our understanding of literary history. Such work may easily be overlooked, and I have chosen this example for that very reason. In dealing with this paper I cannot pretend to be doing full justice to the quality of Dr. Griffith's total contribution, or to be giving a balanced account of any phase of his distinguished career. A just estimate of his great Pope bibliography, which Dobrée in the work I have just referred to calls "masterly," I must leave to other hands. But I believe that Dr. Griffith, practicing scholar that he was, would welcome an attempt to evaluate the place of such a contribution in the workaday academic world. All who knew him will remember that he liked at times to philosophize and moralize a bit about his profession, and we may trust that he would be tolerant of still another small effort to follow the workings of scholarship.

Let us examine briefly the content and purport of the article on the progress pieces.[1] No doubt Dr. Griffith started inductively, moving from the original title of *The Dunciad, The Progress of Dulness.* There were of course many other progress titles, from Donne's *Of the Progresse of the Soule* to Dickens' *Oliver Twist; or, the Parish Boy's Progress.* But does the recurrence of the word mean any more than, say, the recurrence of the word "pleasures" in such titles as *The Pleasures of Melancholy, The Pleasures of Hope,* or *The Pleasures of Memory?* Dr. Griffith gives a thumbnail definition of the kind of progress piece he is chiefly interested in: "an imaginary tour of an allegorical abstraction." He evidently intends this as a fairly close identification of the characteristic eighteenth-century mode, but in various brief references and statements in his article he points toward other modes. Thus he speaks of "the common property of the notions of transmigration and of

[1] I wish to acknowledge my indebtedness to a recent re-examination of the subject in a doctoral dissertation by one of my students, Richard Crider.

the ages of civilization—gold, silver, brass, iron." Or again he remarks, "The conception of history passes from that of a pageant of independent, unconnected scenes to that of a pageant dominated by a principle of continuity, of cause and effect, with each scene alternating its role as effect and cause." He even sees in the biographical progress piece a model for a continuity of character development that suggests the eighteenth-century novel. He also recognizes the presentation of a series of pictures or "characters" as one manifestation of the progress formula. This is not a complete listing of the various types he suggests. Though he possibly underrates the significance of the progress pieces of the eighteenth century in calling them a "fad," he also recognizes in them a pattern by which the didactic poet could set forth in facile and congenial form a history of poetry or of civilization. He appends a list of over ninety progress pieces, to which some additions have been made by Robert A. Aubin, (*Modern Language Notes,* XLIX [1934], 405–407), and Mattie Swayne (*University of Texas Studies in English,* XVI [1936], 84–92).

Among the suggestive notations in Dr. Griffith's article is the application of the progress formula in scientific terms, illustrated by Prior's *Alma,* from which he quotes at length and by which I judge he was honestly puzzled. In dealing with the conflicting theories as to the situation of the soul in relation to the body, Prior makes burlesque use of his "pretty Spanish conceit" that Alma (the soul) enters at the toes and mounts by just degrees through various parts of the body to the brain. His underlying intention is difficult to make out fully, but the progress pattern is probably used here to banter current science and philosophy and also to burlesque the rising mode of scientific or physico-theological poem. Here we need only note how progress in some broad sense shades into the idea of the pervasion of the world of nature by some animating force —the "infusive force of love" in Thomson's *Spring*, for example, or the vitalizing force of warmth and light in *Summer*. The various manifestations or ramifying effects of any entity or force may be broadly called a progress, or the tracing of the chain of being or any sequence of effects might be at least loosely so called. Even more broadly, a journey or quest, a roll-call or catalogue, a prospect or survey may come under this rubric. But after noting how easy it is to extend the term by such applications, we had probably better draw the line and for the purposes of this discussion limit our use of the term to the extensive time sequences of history rather than to apply it to the recurring processes of nature or to the exhibition of a variety of related themes or objects in some spatial scheme. The progress we are talking about represents some magnification or extrapolation of the time span.

Of course the division does not come clean. The connection between the linear and the cyclical, the onward march of history and the recurring spiral, appears strikingly in some recent applications of the term *translatio*. In another context Dr. Samuel Kliger has pointed out the importance for the historical thinking of the Renaissance and the Enlightenment of the idea of the *translatio imperii,* the transfer of empire or supreme political power.[2] The general pattern of the course of empire,

[2] Samuel Kliger, "The Gothic Revival and the German *Translatio*," *Modern Philology,* XLV (1947), 73–103.

inherited from classical and Biblical sources, offers in one of its forms the conception of a succession of incarnated realizations of power, the manifestation of a divine purpose or an eternal form or idea in Troy, in Greece and Rome, and in Britain. This idea sets up a kind of archetype for the progress piece, though its profound implications are not always brought out by the eighteenth century poets. In their practice the chief feature of the progress piece is the allegorical *persona* who moves from point to point or reappears in different contexts—Griffith's "extended tour of an allegorical abstraction." The progress pieces thus fall in, to a large extent, with the strong trend toward allegorical personification. The simple progress in its underlying relationship with *translatio* may be illustrated by some lines in Fenton's *Epistle to Mr. Southerne* (1711):

> Arts have their Empires, and like other States,
> Their Rise and Fall are govern'd by the Fates.
> They, when their Period's measur'd out by Time,
> Transplant their Laurels to another Clime.

This is clearly *translatio;* the Fates and fixed periods of time determine the succession, but as we read of the arts transplanting their laurels and seeking another coast we are likely to think of them as primarily a migrating band of *personae.*

Though Kliger's studies, as far as I know, first brought the idea of *translatio,* at least incidentally, into the discussion of eighteenth-century literature, Aubrey Williams was the first to connect it precisely with the progress piece and in particular with *The Dunciad.* In his important *Pope's "Dunciad": A Study of Its Meaning* (London and Baton Rouge, 1955) he shows the basic importance of the entire pattern for Pope's poem. The main theme is another progress, as if from Troy to Latium, from East to West, that is, in the mock-epic scheme, from the City to the West End. This is of course a *translatio imperii.* The vision of the future displayed in Book VI of the *Aeneid,* Adam's vision in Books XI and XII of *Paradise Lost,* and Theobald's vision in *Dunciad* III all fall into line. Williams moreover connects the underlying idea of historical and geographical continuity in Pope's progress piece with the conception of the *translatio studii,* the transplanting of culture from age to age and country to country.

In itself the idea of succession or sequence is neutral and could be connected variously with mere variety or with theories of decline or of progressive improvement. *Translatio* may almost be reduced to vicissitude, as in the lines just quoted from Fenton or even in such a full-dress progress piece as Thomson's *Liberty:*

> But as from Man to Man, Fate's first Decree,
> Impartial Death the Tide of Riches rolls,
> So States must die and LIBERTY go round.
> (II, 418–420)

But in the full humanistic view vicissitude applies only to the temporal span; above the flux, before and after the flux, is eternal truth, the Platonic idea. *Translatio* in its full meaning points to the *urbs aeterna.* Though empires rise and fall, though culture was alternately developed and destroyed in China, in Alexandria, in the Dark Ages, the entire pattern is cyclical, and represents the recurrence and perpetuation of the ideal. In his presentation of the *translatio studii,* Pope asserted the supreme worth of the ancient heritage, and dwelt on its degeneration as Dulness advanced to new triumphs. But it is only in satire that we are confronted with this complete revision of chaos, this *Götterdämmerung.* In this context even James Thomson, optimistic, benevolent, and progressive though he was, could write in 1730: "All is as dull here as Wit had never been; and the great platonic year predicted by the Dunciad . . . the Millenium of dullness seems to be fast approaching."[3]

In ordinary practice, the progress piece is likely to become a framing scheme for various portrayals and manifestations, separately treated. A deeper continuity, or a final commitment to a doctrine of absolute decline or absolute progress would be too much for the poet. A steady upward and onward advance is seldom asserted, even though the progress piece may seem to be made to order for the purposes of Whig panegyric. In commenting on the fact that Dr. Griffith called the composition of progress pieces a "fad," Richard Crider remarks with commendable caution: "It is tempting to view the historical progress piece as an attempt of the literary community to shape from the materials of history or poetry a myth expressive of England's most valued aspirations at this time, aspirations of intellectual, artistic, social, and imperial achievement. This way of looking at the historical progress piece would help to rescue it from the charge of insignificance, but would perhaps

[3] Alan D. McKillop, ed., *James Thomson: Letters and Documents* (Lawrence, 1958), p. 76. Thomson to Valentine Munbee, October 27, 1730.

tilt the scales too far in the other direction, making the type seem a more weighty accomplishment than it was."

At this point I must become autobiographical for a moment. Pragmatically, an article *is* what it means to other students. Not long after the appearance of Dr. Griffith's article I was undertaking a study of the poet Collins, and I read the following comment with particular interest: "Collins's 'Ode to Liberty' is in outline and in the first half only, almost the same as Thomson's *Liberty,* a progress from Greece through Rome, Florence, Venice, Switzerland, and Holland, to Britain." And again Griffith remarked that Collins used the progress pattern "twice in truncated form, once in full—in the odes to 'Fear' and 'Simplicity' and in the 'Epistle to Hanmer.' " This seemed to me an important point, and in an article on Collins, published in *Studies in Philology* (XX[1923], 1–16), I argue, oversimplifying a good deal, that the progress piece would naturally favor progress in the full sense, and build up to a climax in the present, but that Collins's use of the formula inverts this conclusion and regularly ends with the idea of arrested inspiration, or of the quest of frustrated genius for an unattained ideal. I overworked the idea, though I still think it throws some light on Collins. At any rate, it has done little harm, for no one else has paid any attention to it. Standing by itself this emphasis on Collins's impassioned quest for the inspiration of the ancients gives an unbalanced view of the poet, and makes too much play with romantic *Sehnsucht* (I even mentioned Schiller's *sentimentalische Dichtung*). In the light of recent discussion of the allegorical *persona* in eighteenth century poetry, notably Jean Hagstrum's admirable analysis of Collins's odes in *The Sister Arts* (Chicago, 1958), it now appears that we can get a more adequate understanding of the descriptive and allegorical odes of Collins if we consider them primarily as invocations and visualizations of the *persona,* but also, in close connection with this central principle, as concerned with the successive manifestations of the figure in cultural history. Thus "Fear" begins with a visualization of the central figure and his train, followed by the progress in tragedy. "Pity," which may also be considered a truncated progress piece, likewise combines allegorical visualization and historical manifestation. Among the others, "Liberty" stands somewhat apart in dwelling on the progress rather than on the visualized central figure, and this may be accounted for partly by its special relationship to Thomson's poem. In Collins's poem the conclusion makes the transition from the lost shrine of Liberty in ancient Britain to the beauteous model of the temple still existing in heaven. Here we have the concept of an eternally subsisting ideal which underlies the *translatio* set forth with remarkable clearness. In general the shrine, cell, or temple which figures so prominently in Collins's odes belongs to the static allegorical visualization rather than to the progress pattern; when iconographically elaborated it hardly lends itself to movement through time, but it may be presented as the object of a quest, or even as actually translated from one age to another.

The recently discovered version or rough draft of "Simplicity" shows the original and central importance for the poem of the *persona* conceived of as a statuesque figure in a shrine, and treated as an object of worship and a source of inspiration.[4]

> O Chaste Unboastfull Guide
> O'er all my Heart preside
> And midst my Cave in breathing Marble wrought
> In sober Musing near
> With Attic Robe appear
> And charm my sight and prompt my temprate thought.

The imagery is not entirely clear, but in the earlier version we find the theme of the power or influence of the "modest maid" in the various arts; she is explicitly invoked as "Thrice Gentle Guide of each exalted Art." The emphasis is originally on the concurrent manifestations in the arts rather than on the march down the ages. The brief progress in the historical sense is added in the final version, from Greece to Rome and now perhaps to some "temp'rate Vale" (wherever it may be) which the poet seeks—a pastoral version of the invocation in the earlier version:

> Return sweet Maid at length
> In all thy Ancient strength
> And bid our Britain hear thy Grecian song.

The progress pattern is prominent in the final version, but it is presented as a retreat or withdrawal. Where is the shrine of Simplicity now? There is a parallel here to the transfer or hypostasis of the shrine of Liberty already mentioned.

[4] William Collins, *Drafts & Fragments of Verse,* ed. J. S. Cunningham (Oxford, 1956), pp. 1–3.

I must conclude with a brief consideration of the diploma piece in the whole genre, Gray's "Progress of Poesy." The second part of the poem is a signal example of the pattern: poesy progresses from the primitive state in northern climes and tropical forests through Greece and Latium to England; then comes the English sequence—Shakespeare, Milton, Dryden, and Gray himself. The conclusion, expressing the idea of arrested or imperfect inspiration which we have seen in Collins, asserts the poet's quest rather than actual achievement. Without analyzing this progress in full detail, let us ask how, if at all, the opening section connects with it and leads into it. Gray's original title was "The Powers of Poetry." If we think of the basic plan as the expression of diverse manifestations of these powers, we can see that under this caption we might get a series of instances or modes which would invite comparison with the progress structure. In the opening section, then, we have in succession the figure of the powerful and picturesque stream of music (equated with poetry), the "power of harmony to calm the turbulent sallies of the soul," and lastly its expression in the allied art of the dance. The figure of the stream presents the idea of the continuity of the power of poetry in its various styles, whether as an animating rill, a broad majestic river, or a roaring cataract.[5] This is a generalized description, full of movement, rather than a static pic-

[5] Horace uses the river symbol for Pindar's full and majestic style (*Odes,* IV, ii), and Thomson applies it to the Greek language itself (*Liberty,* II, 257–260). There is, moreover, a particularly close connection between Gray's lines and Thomson's description of the course of the Nile (*Summer,* ll. 812–821).

torial presentation. As in one of Thomson's descriptions, though in more condensed form, a generalized force of nature is substituted for a *persona.* In contrast to this we have in the epode of the first section the central figure of Cytherea (Aphrodite), attended by Loves, Sports, Pleasures, and Graces. Though the dance of Cytherea is a progress only in the limited sense of triumphal pageant, it falls in with the larger movement of the poem. Throughout the first section, even though we do not have a formal historical sequence with the time dimension emphasized, each division embodies motion which we may call poetry in action, and which may be taken to stand for or to be incorporated in the infinite extension of the power of poetry.

The transition from the varied manifestations of the power in the first section to the historical succession in the second is effected by the introduction of the time dimension in the form of a dawn after darkness sequence (ll. 49–57). This launches us fairly into the history. Admirable and memorable though Gray's lines are, there is a decline of momentum in the second part, and a less effective multiplication of symbols and *personae*. Yet, with the exception of the inferior strophe on Shakespeare, images of flight and exalted movement still prevail, and the impetus of the opening is never entirely lost. Jean Hagstrum has given a thorough analysis of this ode in terms of pictorial effect.[6] In order to balance this account, I would add only that Gray's translation of a central concept of the power of poetry into what we may call process and progress rep-

[6] *The Sister Arts* (Chicago, 1958), pp. 301–306.

resents a magnificent attempt to take seriously the tradition we have been considering.

In pursuing inquiries of this kind, we should remember our point of origin. I would in conclusion describe Dr. Griffith's article as effective and suggestive, as helpfully exploratory, as carrying much more weight than its directness and simplicity would intimate to the casual reader. This is what Browning calls fishing up the murex, the shellfish that gives the purple dye; or, if we wish to draw on Tennyson also, we may say, "Most can raise the flowers now, for all have got the seed." Yet he serves well who first sets forth for our consideration the operative idea.

ALAN D. MCKILLOP

TEACHING OF ENGLISH AS A PROFESSION

IT IS BOTH an honor and a pleasure to speak before an organization founded so many years ago by the late Professor Griffith, and especially to speak at a meeting designed to honor his memory. He never forgot what on an occasion like this we may well remember, namely, that we are all members of a learned profession and thus have professional obligations and responsibilities. One of several college presidents under whom I have served used to say that it is almost impossible to get a professor to think seriously about the nature of his job. A by-product of this view was that since the professor could, or would, not formulate theories and policies in his job, that function might well devolve upon the president. He then becomes the policy maker, the staff officer, and the professor is the field officer, facing the enemy in the classroom.

I do not like this sort of thinking, and believe that every professor should concern himself with the theory as well as the practice of his own job, focusing upon his own job, perhaps, rather than on that of his colleagues. If we do this we shall have first of all to consider certain inescapable questions: 1. What as professors do we really profess? 2. How do we fit ourselves for our job? 3. How can we most effectively perform the job? and, 4. last, if we believe that in the long run a well-trained scholar makes the best teacher, how shall we define true scholarship as it applies to us individually?

These are large questions, and today briefly we shall have to deal only with large general answers.

Obviously we profess to know something—perhaps even a lot—about English literature. We read and speak English intelligently, so we think, and we have gifts of interpreting masterpieces of literature. Colleagues and others will differ in their estimate of our abilities—the abilities themselves will vary greatly, perhaps, at different times in our professional careers.

We all think we can write competently, but it is no secret to any American who reads English reviews of American books that the English think that, on the whole, professors in the U.S.A. write rather badly. However, if you want to lose a good professorial friend, simply try to tell him that he writes badly. Such opinions are what make enemies for editors of our learned journals. There are professors who will hardly forgive an editor for making obvious corrections in grammar. I should hardly dare to tell any single professorial victim that he writes badly, but here with a lot of you ready to unsheath your knives, I must confess that I am inclined to agree with the English critics. But I see an extenuating reason, which they apparently do not concern themselves with. The reason is that we like to crowd our scholarly canvases with complex factual details that would require something like Edward Gibbon's skill—and there has never been but one Gibbon—to marshal our facts gracefully. The English seldom get tangled up in that trap, because they like to concern themselves less with factual information than with the pleasant realms of personal opinion. I have sometimes thought that the English should be discouraged from the production of books of reference. Leave that to the Germans or to the Americans, and insist on inclusiveness rather than on suave elegance. The general superiority of the Baedeker guide books over the chattiness of the so-called Blue Guides is a fair exhibit in the case. Most of us have had the experience of listening to distinguished Englishmen who come to us as lecturers, and the solid American opinion certainly is that their remarks may be elegantly phrased, but that very little is being said. But all this flattering unction may well be thinly applied: we need to get rid of the idea that since we are presenting "new" material, we can simply fling it in the face of the reader. Good writing is in part the result of practice, and we all need practice. We must profess that we write well until we can demonstrate the fact.

HOW DO WE PREPARE ourselves for our chosen profession? I do not here intend to indulge in the pleasant sport of baiting the requirements for the Ph.D. degree. No mechanical system is ever perfect. Sir William Craigie used to say that a professor of English ought to be able to read and explain English of any period. This is easily said, but Craigie and everyone else must admit that explanations can be onerous, if not tedious. It is, however, an ideal to shoot at. One may note that the ideal cannot properly be attained without a considerable knowledge of literatures in other languages, and this fact should be kept in mind in shaping the preparation for our work. Our preparation involves of course an endless amount of reading. Long years ago a German scholar defined training with the words: *lesen; viel lesen; immer viel lesen.* Yet we must keep in mind the old joke about the man who read so much that he had no time left for thinking.

ONCE TRAINED AND EMPLOYED, how do we perform? (Training, evidently, must be always a continuing process: it continues throughout one's performing career.) Once in conversation with an officer in a medical school, I ventured to speak enviously of how much more they were able to do in screening candidates for admission to medical schools than any English department could do for prospective graduate students. "Yes," he relied, with some irritation, "we screen them, they come, and after years of education they go out, and it's absolutely impossible to tell whether or not they will make reputable physicians." One can apparently get an M.D., or in our case a Ph.D., and still not be competent for his chosen job. There is no conceivable system that has ever been able to make a silk purse out of—you know what.

I have great sympathy for the young Ph.D. who enters on his first five years in teaching. Most of them do well—I trust very well. One must, however, warn them: "The first job is not so difficult to get: it's the second one that you have to look out for." The young doctor comes out of graduate school tired of the strain of getting the degree, and ready to relax and take life easily. I once heard a candidate in Classics remark, "If I ever get this thesis done and get the degree, I'll never look at another book as long as I live." One recognizes the mood. But these first five years are crucially formative. If one relaxes then, one seldom hits a real stride later. The young man has to make good as a teacher, not flashily but solidly, and has to keep alive intellectually and creatively. My next best piece of advice to the young man is that he make close friends only with colleagues who are both alert and productive—men whom one can look up to always.

A good teacher is one who organizes his classwork clearly and attractively. He will never think with regard to his captive audience, "I am giving them the true facts of the case, and if they don't listen, it's their loss." The teacher must win his audience and not bore it. It always did me good on rare occasions to sit with the class while someone else talked to us for fifty minutes. I learned a lot that way—about how uncomfortable hard chairs can be, and about the need for a change-of-pace effect in the middle of a lecture. The teacher must speak well: I have more than once told a graduate seminar, "What you people need most in the world is some training in speech." We all ought to be able to read poetry aloud in a sympathetic and sensible fashion. In his early period of training as well as later the professor should often practice reading aloud when alone. This ability, like playing a musical instrument or taking pictures with a camera, will deteriorate if not exercised.

The young doctor must also practice writing, especially writing for publication. There are a few places where the young man may be told, "We value good teaching, and don't care whether you ever publish anything or not." Such places, sincere as they may be, must be eyed with suspicion. Administrations and policies change suddenly at times, and some day the young man—possibly no longer young—may be, as we say, "let out" because he has never published anything. I have known good men to be thus trapped and unfairly treated years after the first policy against publication had been stated.

There is, of course, much talk of excessive emphasis on publication as a criterion for advancement in our profession. A long-time Ph.D. who is known as a valued administrator and as author of a few novels that few have ever read—and as author of little else—summed up the need in a sentence: "An administration wants its professors to be judged by their peers and not merely by a lot of undergraduates." We can be judged by our peers only if we are seen intellectually by them outside the classroom. Publication in many institutions—it ought to be so in all—may include creative writing as well as what we normally call scholarly writing. The danger of relying on creative writing is that judgments about it vary even more than they do about the factual data, inferences from which constitute "scholarship." If a fact is established *and has mean-*

ing, it is more surely evaluated as achievement than are imaginative fantasies, about which opinions are notoriously subjective.

I always advise young doctors not to be flattered by seeing themselves in demand as errand boys for the Department or even for a dean. Often five years of such service are rewarded by the old heave ho. "He's a good kid," they say, "but he's just scattering himself about and getting nowhere." Amid so many gambles, however, it is no wonder the young man takes the wrong turning.

The trouble is that faculties have no realistic or objective conception of the sort of men they want: they need to consider more carefully than they have ever done the qualifications that they regard as essential. I have never loved faculty meetings, but I remember one with gusto. There was once a very distinguished professor of Latin, who in a dull faculty meeting made a speech that I shall never forget. He began smoothly as follows: "If a young man should come to me and ask,'What qualities must I cultivate in order to secure a permanent place in this university,' I should tell him . . ." and from there on he presented a gorgeous and impossible array of *sine-qua-nons.* I went home and to myself burlesqued the speech by saying to an imaginary man, "You should have the wisdom of Solomon, the reasoning powers of Aristotle, an encyclopaedic store of information, the personal integrity and charm of St. Paul, and the overriding determination of Adolf Hitler. Then you might have a chance." All that most departments know is that they want the *best.* Universities want better men than grow on trees, and so are often in a state of frustration as to what constitutes a good teacher or scholar. Tangible prescriptions will be difficult to come by, but in handling personnel problems we have much to learn from big business. We might see the need, as business does, of doing personnel training for our young employees. If they know where we want them to go, they will normally be eager to please; but someone has to supervise their efforts. Much can be done by friendly supervision and interest even with older members of a staff.

When I went to the University of Chicago as a graduate student, a newly imported chairman, William Allen Nitze, headed the Romance Department. In my mind he is still the ideal chairman. He had inherited in the department some full professors who were, just to be realistic, almost broken-down old war horses. He did a real personnel job with them. One he persuaded to edit an important Old French text, another to become a famous grammarian, and others to turn out distinguished biographies or critical studies. The result was that in a matter of a few years his department was generally recognized as the best department of Romance Languages in the country. This sort of thing can happen; but it is difficult, and increasingly so, if one expects chairmen of departments to become personnel counsellors. The trouble is that there are too many deans and other faculty crackpots who believe in education by legislation: faculties lay down so many rules that a chairman has as his chief and time-consuming function the duty of seeing that the rules are all observed; that all the printed forms (all subject to revision overnight) are filled out at the proper date, and that the daily routine goes on smoothly. The situation is so bad in these respects that one is driven to wonder if we should not be better off if we never conferred any degrees but simply concentrated on the acquisition and diffusion of something like learning. The abolition of degrees is of course an insanely Utopian notion—designed merely to give the topless towers of academic legislation a shake and a shudder.

Less fantastic, more practical, should be another matter. Very likely everyone here has said or has heard a colleague say wistfully that he would like a job in a good university where he would have a lot of time in which to do his own work. I have taught in good universities, but there are none, absolutely none, that grant a man time in which to do his own work in research or what have you. The time has to be taken, to be "made" somehow. There should be for men at the top more research professorships: there are now very few in the field of English, although they are most desirable in a field where encouragement is necessary to stimulate men to something more than just plodding along in a "service" routine. From the instructor up to the sixty-year-old professor, time for research or writing has to be stolen from other academic assignments, especially from teaching. For the young man that is a very bad situation—as it is for everyone. What lack of time does to one's desire for human existence, for golf or bridge, is a matter that can be left only to the individual conscience.

The full professor is burdened with the task of supervising Ph.D. theses or with other time-consuming assignments. We need to campaign strongly for recognition of these tasks as meriting a release from teaching or at least from the intolerable amount of committee work that administrators love to impose. I have been in hopes that the recent scandals about mills or factories that will produce a Ph.D. thesis for a candidate at a cost of from three to eight thousand dollars (I believe those are the figures mentioned in the newspapers)—I have hoped, I say, that this situation, rare as it certainly is, might furnish leverage to secure more time for the conscientious and tedious work of supervising theses. Only by such relief can we in the already overcrowded graduate schools of English make sure of the thoroughness of our work and the quality of our product. If a professor is actively supervising more than two theses a year, he ought to be compelled to take a reduction in his teaching load and be exempt from committee work. Especially is this true if the supervision of a thesis involves correspondence with a candidate teaching at another institution. Such supervision by remote control is at best not very desirable.

A totally different type of advice may well be bestowed on professors—especially on such as, rightly or wrongly, think very highly of themselves. They need to cultivate tolerance and good nature. But surely, you hasten to protest, "We are not to be tolerant of low standards?" and I reply, "Certainly not of your own low standards, if any; but for those of your colleagues—well, give it a try." It is natural for each of us to believe in his own work and in its superior importance. The corollary that the work of others is somehow inferior has to be resisted. I have seldom known a professor who *talked loudly* about the need of high standards on the part of others who did not neglect to scrutinize his own. He is so sure of his own standards that he wants all his students passed for degrees without question. Certainly we must work for high standards, but peacefully, quietly, and in a conciliatory, not a hostile, fashion. Contempt for the standards of others if publicized does less good than you may think. In breeding ill nature it possibly does as much harm as would even a mistaken tolerance. Somehow we must establish more objective standards and maintain them rigorously.

There is another, different angle to this matter of tolerance. I shall never forget a conversation with a dean who at a public luncheon addressed some thinking-out-loud to my left ear. He had just before lunch been bored by a pest who held at some length that one's appreciation of music depends entirely on the state of one's diaphragm. The dean was, to me, sincere if not perfectly tactful. "I don't think," he said, "that when it comes to making appointments the English department is the hardest one to get a candidate approved in. I think music is worse. They do so many different things. One man thinks, 'We have never had a distinguished performer, and such an appointment would make for good public relations.' Another thinks that for academic purposes a musicologist is essential. Another wants someone to teach composition, and still another thinks that conducting makes a distinguished career, and we need a man who can teach conducting." The poor dean was out of intellectual breath, and was relieving his inmost feelings. Consequently I did not counter by saying that the same problems come up in English. We do many things with our far-flung peripheries of journalism, creative writing, speech, and what have you—all of which I like to see roofed in the same shelter as the teaching of literary history, of criticism, of expertise in Shakespeare and James Joyce. Fundamentally we have to envisage the creative, the critical, and the historical functions, and they sometimes prove uneasy bedfellows. The pot under these circumstances must be slow to call anything black. We must tolerate many diverse functions.

One needs to be tolerant also of personal limitations. I could name one very able professor who was so notoriously intolerant of everything about the university where he passed most of his academic life that over a period of years, because of his thorny personality, his resignation would have been welcome. In the outside world he was famous. And yet in his own university, though well-known for his scholarly writing, he had no standing at all. It must have been a painful state for all concerned.

To repeat: we do not perform at our best without being able to perceive the failings of others in charity and to cultivate something in the way of self-criticism. Our ambition is to be a success both in the classroom and among our colleagues outside the classroom.

AND SO WE MAY TURN to consider perhaps the most important question: "What is the nature of the scholarship desirable in our profession?" One gets differing notions of it. Not many years ago the president of a distinguished university journeyed some miles to address the students of another institution on an occasion designed to honor scholarship. All I know of what he said in his speech comes from the one sentence that was syndicated from it by the public press. The harmless remark, so widely disseminated, was that "The life of a scholar is a lonely one, but it may be very rewarding." To news reporters, who are so busy in the teeming world of affairs, this remark evidently seemed an intellectual gem, and of course it does represent a common and persistent view of scholarship. As far back as 1778 Dr. Johnson merely varied the tune a bit when he remarked of a man whom he did not cherish, "A mere antiquarian is a rugged being." We again get an aspect of this stock figure in a little poem by Vachel Lindsay.[1] Let me say it for you:

The mouse that gnawed the oak-tree down
Began his task in early life.
He kept so busy with his teeth
He had no time to take a wife.

He gnawed and gnawed through sun and rain
When the ambitious fit was on,
Then rested in the sawdust till
A month of idleness had gone.

He did not move about to hunt
The coteries of mousie-men.
He was a snail-paced, stupid thing
Until he cared to gnaw again.

The mouse that gnawed the oak-tree down,
When that tough foe was at his feet—
Found in the stump no angel-cake,

[1] "The Mouse That Gnawed the Oak-Tree Down," from *Collected Poems* by Vachel Lindsay, Copyright 1914 by The Macmillan Company, renewed 1942 by E. C. Lindsay, and used with the permission of The Macmillan Company.

Nor buttered bread, nor cheese, nor meat—
The forest roof let in the sky,
"This light is worth the work," said he.
"I'll make this ancient swamp more light,"
And started on another tree.

This is both the poet's and the great world's idea of the awkward, unthanked idealist, whom we call (sometimes) a scholar. There is little use in trying to show such people other aspects of his character. If the scholar is lonely, he is perhaps complacent in what has been called the solid satisfaction of self-applause. If he is rugged, he at least is spared the consciousness of that fact: he is perhaps excessively intent, so people insist, on his own work of gnawing at tough ignorance.

For a *slightly* less conventional characterization we may start with the proposition that essentially the scholar is a man afflicted with an incurable passion for knowledge. That perhaps is all there is to it at the start. The scholar's ideas as to rewards, if he has any, are extremely variable but are normally idealistic. His reward will never be wealth, and at heart he can never be really lonely, for, rightly constituted, he can echo with enthusiasm the Elizabethan poet who sang, "My mind to me a kingdom is." The scholar has his subjects, which he commands with satisfaction like a monarch: he has no need for small people or small talk.

So far from being lonely the scholar nowadays rather has to fight for privacy. He is never isolated. *Fortune* magazine—to see how the real world wags—has printed an article on "Team Research." It ended with the somewhat plaintive query, "What, then, becomes of the individual researcher?"

The point of the article seemed to be that if a scholar wishes to be widely recognized as such and especially if he wishes to enjoy lush subsidies from our larger foundations, he must sell to his chosen foundation a project neatly tailored to require a total cost running into six figures together with the services of a team of workers. If the present day researcher works in an ivory tower, the tower may well be a skyscraper; it will be equipped with a group or team of researchers, two or three attractive typists at least, and it will hardly be a spot devoted to loneliness. If the president who thinks scholars are lonely should drop into one or two buildings of his own university, he would find more than one professor has a team of assistants feeding facts into a hopper from which semiannually emerges a book.

Quite apart from all this opulence even the meagre individual scholar, while at work, can escape loneliness by being affable with his colleagues or by a thriving long-range correspondence with some remote scholar who is interested in his work. One professor conducts a sympathetic, but argumentative, correspondence with a learned lady in Palermo; another tries to be courteous to a stupid critic in Calcutta. From various points of view the scholar's world is a widely small one, closely knit by argumentative or factual ties. There is of course a type of secretive scholar who fears anticipation by some rival more active than himself. This type may be lonely, but he is moderately rare. The individual scholar, as compared with the team worker, in my opinion has the great advantage of doing and controlling his own work; but the team-researcher, if he has a sincere thirst for knowledge and not merely an exhibitionist complex, can surely, with his hired help, achieve distinguished success. But we needn't be afraid of loneliness: nowadays that is a luxury unattainable. Organizers, colleagues, faculty committees, and at times even undergraduates make it so.

The best antidote for ruggedness is doubtless a wife. If the scholar himself has no small talk, the wife will cheerfully fill in for him; and if properly trained, she refrains from advertising his ruggedness: she may even soften or obscure it. The wife who is also a scholar is a true helpmate. Any dull summer's day you can see such couples side by side in the British Museum poring over volumes, fascinated for hours. I once leaned over such a couple and said, "My slogan for scholars is a wife in every library." In cases where such proliferation is not quite practicable, even one wife has obvious advantages. Loneliness is nonexistent: ruggedness can be cured.

But the scholar is a specialist. A great deal of talk about overspecialization is nowadays current. Any news reporter who specializes only in disaster or crime, can see that specialization is bad, and he will publicize talk against it as regularly as he will talk about using slang. Few critics deny the need for experts in our present mechanized civilization, but many deplore the normal scholar's abstraction from what we like to call polite learning. By a doubtless unwarrantable oversimplification one may generalize that the Germans believe in *expertise* whereas the English hardly do. Fifty years ago a distinguished American educator was talking with an English cabinet minister at a time when in England they were having a big coal strike. "Well," said the harassed minister, "what do you think is wrong with the British government?" The instantaneous reply was: "Too many amateurs running it." He proceeded to explain that at the moment the world's greatest expert on coal mining, a German, was in London, "and," he added, "none of you is aware of his existence." German influence on American education has now wisely declined—probably even disappeared; and a curious amateurish imitation of England has crept in. What we might best learn from English universities—their simplified methods of administration—we seem totally to neglect.

Really top scholars are by no means always narrow, overspecialized men. I'm not thinking of remote Titans like Leonardo da Vinci, but rather (to be specific) of the two best minds which it was briefly my privilege to glimpse. One was that of the great bacteriologist and surgeon, Dr. Welch of Johns Hopkins, whose interest in history, literature, and art certainly kept pace with his highly specialized medical work. The other was Professor A. A. Michaelson of the University of Chicago, who was the first or almost the first American physicist to win a Nobel prize. Michaelson played the violin well, painted charming water colors, and was an insatiate reader of novels in Spanish and French. Ambition toils after such minds in vain—but it can toil.

Scholarship requires data, facts, much as a motor requires fuel; but if the facts do not turn to fuel, they become merely a clogging sediment. The encyclopaedic mind, stuffed with diversity of fact, does not make the ideal scholar. Encyclopaedias are wonderfully useful things, much as indexes are. They serve to illustrate the poet's observation of

How index-learning turns no student pale
Yet holds the eel of science by the tail.

But facts, like the coin of the realm, are useful only when they circulate or fulfill a specific function. Skill as much as fact is requisite for scholarship: both are essential. What the scholar chiefly knows is how to do things—and what things are worth doing. His work is an act of faith and of courage. Oak trees are tough. He has a task to do, and he pursues it with devotion and patience. I once heard a professor say, "The man who gets on in the world is the one who invests in his career." What he gets out of his career is at first a minor question. He must invest time, money, and all that he has of intelligent effort. In concrete terms this frequently means the choice between investing in a trip to the British Museum or buying a car. The choice is painful, but for most of us inevitable.

The professor spoke of "getting on," and you will recall that the orator already quoted spoke glowingly of rewards. In one sense scholarship resembles virtue: its rewards are intangibles. To the world they sometimes look like sawdust; but the mouse saw his product as light.

Strange as it may seem to some, the real scholar enjoys his rugged work much as an athlete enjoys his game. Scholarship is a game: it plays miniature knowledge against mammoth ignorance, and the outcome is frequently uncertain. The game thus takes on a heroic aspect, and the scholar rather fancies himself as hero. He thinks joyfully of his Homeric, or rather Tennysonian, predecessor, Ulysses, who will not become an aged idler, but will sail off into unknown seas, not knowing if he may ever return or what he may find in his further aged wanderings:

> It may be we shall touch the Happy Isles
> And see the great Achilles, whom we knew.

It seems all a sporting chance—animated by the thirst for and belief in exploration and dominated by a heroic spirit. How different that spirit is from the frustrated mood of our own day when our chief poet tells us—

> We shall not cease from exploration
> And the end of all our exploring
> Will be to arrive where we started
> And to know the place for the first time.

There is, or used to be, a notion that persons lost in a wilderness are likely to circle about and presently arrive where they had started. It is to be hoped that such is not the fate of our century, and that our explorations may meet with somewhat more by way of tangible success. An antidote to frustration may lie in heroically daring intellectual labor, and one may take heart from the symbolic Victorian Ulysses, who was ready to believe that by voyaging in unknown seas one might gain new light on the human lot. In any case it is such lofty courage as that of men like Ulysses, actuated by his determination,

> To strive, to seek, to find, and not to yield . . .

that makes scholarship the noblest of all games.

GEORGE SHERBURN

THE GREAT TORCH RACE[1]

If I had ingenuity enough, I should try this afternoon to put together for you an account of the contents of the Wrenn Library. The task is impossible, and any attempt would be unendurably cataloguy and dry. In its stead, you are cordially invited to visit the Library, which is open daily from nine to five, when Miss Ratchford or I will gladly outline for you what is there, with the books before your eyes.

Let me ask you now to give your imagination play, and build before your mind's eye a picture, which I shall call The Great Torch Race. Let me sketch in three panels of it—

[1] An address delivered at the dedication of the Wrenn Library on March 26, 1920, by Reginald Harvey Griffith, and first printed by The University of Texas at that time.

something concerning the founders of libraries, something of the greatness of books, something of the place and opportunity of Texas—and you, if you please, in your imagination build the rest of the picture.

The ancient Greeks had an athletic contest which they called a torch race. Each contestant carried a torch, and the winner was the first to reach the goal with his torch still alight. A variation of the game was the relay race, in which a companion seized the lighted torch from the spent runner and continued the race. This ancient game has more than once done service as a figure of speech to symbolize the progress of civilization through the world's history. In the great march upward from the night of ignorance, the leaders of men have been thought of as each lighting a torch, carrying it high in life, and at death entrusting it to the hands of a younger companion, to be borne by successive hands forever onward towards the goal. Such leaders have been many—as numberless as are ideas among men. And their torches in the pageant have flamed with colors innumerable.

It is of only a very few such bearers of torches in the great and lucent race that I ask you to allow me to speak—especially of book collectors, founders of libraries.

The library at Oxford University boasts two very early friends. But their benefactions—alas!—perished in the savagery of *subsequent* wars. Richard de Bury was the author of the *Philobiblon*, the "Book Lover." His ambition was to assure assistance to the whole University out of his books. He provided the ordinary texts and commentaries for the students, and was extremely anxious that they should be instructed in

Greek and the languages of the East. Rules for the use of the books were strict. A raw student, he said, would treat a book as roughly as if it were a pair of shoes, would stick in straws to keep his place, and would very likely eat fruit or cheese over one page and set a cup of ale on the other, or impudently scribble across the text, or try his pen on a blank space; "and all these negligences," he adds, "are wonderfully injurious to books."

Duke Humphrey, third son of King Henry IV and brother to King Henry V, Falstaff's "Prince Hal," is often spoken of as the founder of the library. His whole family cared for books and were generous to the University, but Humphrey, called the Good Duke Humphrey, was especially so. His gifts were acknowledged to be "an almost unspeakable blessing." When his books arrived, "the general joy knew no bounds"; and the name "Duke Humphrey's Library" was given to the general assemblage of the University's books.

Sir Thomas Bodley did more than either or both of these. He won a great reputation as an ambassador, and Queen Elizabeth would gladly have retained him in political service. But in 1597 he had grown weary of affairs of state. He determined them to give his means and himself for the rest of his life to the service of books. He would make the library at Oxford one of the world's greatest. Here are his own quaint words: "I concluded at the last to set up my staff at the library door in Oxon. I found myself furnished with such four kinds of aids as, unless I had them all, I had no hope of success. For without some kind of knowledge, without some purse-ability to go through with the charge, without good store of friends to further the design, and without special good leisure to follow such a work, it could not but have proved a vain attempt." He supplied funds and had agents buying books in all parts of Europe. He refitted the chamber for the library, supplying cases and tables and chains—he was extraordinarily careful about the chains, with which the books were chained to the shelves. His enthusiasm was so great that friends were glad to assist him with gifts of precious volumes. From his home county of Devon, Dudley Carleton wrote in a gossipy letter: "Every man bethinks himself how by some good book or other he may be written in the scroll of the benefactors." When King James I visited Bodley at the library, he said: "If I were not a King I would be an University-man, and if it were so that I must be a prisoner I would desire no other durance than to be chained in that library with so many noble authors." Sir Thomas lived and wrought on till 1613. The wonderful library, the Bodleian, exists at Oxford now; and to this time the University offers public thanks for Bodley's generosity yearly upon his calendar-day.

The greatness of the library at Cambridge University dates from the year 1715, when Dr. Richard Bentley, greatest of all English scholars, prevailed upon King George I to donate to Cambridge, at a cost of 6,000 guineas (equivalent to about $300,000 now), the books of Bishop Moore of the diocese of Ely. Bishop Burnet writes that the library was a treasure beyond what anyone would think the life and labor of a man could compass.

One of the most interesting collections at Cambridge is the gift of Samuel Pepys. Of the garrulous Pepys it is hard to say whether he will live longest because he wrote the most delightful diary in the world, or because he was founder of the British navy—the wall, first of wood, now of steel, around the liberties of England—or because he collected books. His penchant was for plays, street ballads, and the ephemeral literature of his day. He willed his books to Magdalene College, Cambridge, and there they are now, in the same cases that stood in Pepys's own home and placed on the shelves in the very order he himself chose, the tall books at the back showing over the tops of the small books in front. He made a catalogue, which he called "titleing" his volumes. One of the pleasant pictures of the Diary is of how he himself, and the very young and pretty Mistress Pepys, and Deb Willett, the young serving maid (also pretty, he naively relates) were busy one evening until midnight "titleing" the books.

Robert Harley, Earl of Oxford, and intimate friend of Pope and Swift and Prior, was a prince among collectors. The Harleian library contained 50,000 books, a huge body of manuscripts, and an incredible number of pamphlets. Dr. Johnson has described the contents. The Earl had the rarest books of all countries, languages, and sciences; thousands of fragments, some a thousand years old; vellum books; a great collection of Bibles, and editions of all the first printed books, classics and those of English writers printed by Caxton, Wynkyn de Worde, Pynson, Berthelet, Rastell, and Grafton; the greatest number of pamphlets and English portraits of any other person; original letters of eminent persons as many as would fill 200 volumes; all the collections of Humphrey Wanley, Stow, Sir Simonds D'Ewes, Prynne, Bishop Stillingfleet, John Bagford, Le Neve, and the flower of a hundred other libraries. Most of the library was scattered. But the manuscripts were purchased by the nation in 1753; and they, with the scientific collection and the books of Dr. Hans Sloane, bought at the same time, were the beginning of the British Museum.

Book collecting might well seem to be one of the best guarantees of long life, for most collectors have lived to a ripe old age. Better still, it may be said of them as a class what Dr. Johnson said of one of them: He lived more in the broad sun of life than any other man I ever knew. But doubtless the founders who have left libraries to be sources of knowledge and wisdom and joy to after-comers will rejoice most in the ineffable pleasure they bestow. The eminent scholar Heinsius said, when entering the library at the University of Leyden: "In the very bosom of eternity among all these illustrious souls I take my seat."

What are the books to be desired for a library? First, of course, those the world generally agrees upon as its great books. Is there any underlying principle, any quality shared in common by them? Here is a partial answer for consideration.

Humanity thinks most highly of those men who give the best reasons for thinking highly of humanity. The human race wishes to believe in itself—in its own dignity, worth, and importance. The thinker who bears credible testimony to such worth is acclaimed. And those authors are reckoned greatest whose testimony does most to convince us of the superlative importance of man.

Test this answer for a few moments.

The Bible let us put aside, for it is the thinking of a people, not of one man; and by most Christians it is held to be of divine origin, not human. The sum of its whole message, however, is the worth and eternal importance of every individual soul.

Homer writes of the ten-years war that racked Greece and ruined Troy, of the passions and ambitions, the greatness and littleness of man. He tells of the deities who left high Olympus to come down and help in the battle of man. You do not believe in those gods and goddesses. Perhaps Homer himself did not wholly believe in them. Yet they represented to him and to the listeners to his story the highest forces they could conceive in the whole realm of the universe. If, then, these greatest of all forces assisted in the affairs of men, some on the one side, some on the other, how great, how important, how dignified and worthy must Man be!

Dante journeyed through hell and purgatory and heaven, seeing in those vast confines the fates of men. For him they represented all that is at all after the end of this short life. But Eternal Might and Love created these regions for men's souls. How great, then, how worthy the souls of men!

Shakespeare presents his evidence of the majesty, the excellence, and the weakness too of man in a different way. He conceives of the passions of men,—the fears, hates, jealousies, envies, the loyalties, self-sacrifices, loves—on an enormous scale, tempestuous, mountainous, and puts them in movement within the soul of man. Like a tropical storm they pass through. How immense in its capacity for suffering, for joy, is the soul in which such forces have room to move! And then—wonderful to contemplate!—at the end of each great play, when the storm has blown upon and dissipated the miasmas of a sick and stagnant moral atmosphere, the great dramatist shows the breaking through of a sweetness of light, like a sunset, giving promise of a fairer day to follow, when justice and right shall more nearly rule the world so late disturbed. Do we believe him? Does not his evidence persuade us to a belief in the worth and dignity of the human soul?

Milton tells the story of the Loss of Eden and the consequent sin and sickness and evil besetting us all around. You may not believe in the dire dungeons of darkness made visible that he paints, or in the conclaves of fallen angels, or the other means by which he weaves his ideas into a story. But here is the heart and core of his conception. He thinks of God and his angels as embodying the infinite forces of Good, and Satan and his cohorts as embodying, personifying, the infinite forces of Evil. These infinite forces are in constant conflict. And the reward of victory in the ever-renewed battle is the soul of Adam, the soul of every man, your soul, my soul. But not alone is man's soul the reward, the guerdon of this battle; each individual soul is the battle ground where the contest is fought out. If, then, soul is both ground of battle between the greatest thinkable forces in the universe, and the prize of victory, how worthy, how dignified, how great that soul must be!

You nor any other person will cavil at the gathering together of the great books. But some may ask, Why add the books of little men, the more commonplace writers? Such persons are not so thoroughgoingly drastic as the Caliph

Omar, who destroyed the library of Alexandria, reasoning thus: If the books here agree with the Koran, they are useless, and should be destroyed; if they disagree, they are wicked and ought to be destroyed. No—but still—Why the lesser authors, whose books have not been reprinted and consequently can be come at only in the great libraries? To understand the world, to know ourselves, we need the lesser as well as the greater ones. By as much as the great man has personality, individuality, genius, by so much does he rise above the general level and fail to represent the average man. The eighteenth century discovered the common man. Out of the throes of its revolutions democracy was born. And democracy is today the world's great throbbing *yes* to the ancient question, "Am I my brother's keeper?" In this brotherhood of man, which lifts all men up, not drags any down, how can one keep his brother or be kept, except he knows the moods, the thoughts, the needs, the weakness, the latent greatness too in the commonalty, in the hearts of common men!

The ideal library should have Terence's words for its motto: Nothing that concerns men is alien to me.

Now a library is not of a university. Far from it! Yet the library, and the use made of it—the study of the thoughts and habits and deeds of men, of the spirits of nations, of the soul of man—are the surest index to the excellence of the institution.

What of Texas? What have we? How do we compare with others? What is fitting and becoming? What may we expect and try to have?

We are not without our torch-bearers, our own helpful

collectors. Written in "the scroll of the benefactors" are names you are familiar with: the picturesque Sir Swante Palm, whose name is on many a book housed here behind us; and Ashbel Smith; Miss Florence Brooke; and Henry P. Hilliard, who has done much for our collection of Southern authors. Major Littlefield has given with both hands, so to speak. His is the "purseability" that is enabling his "good store of friends," Professors Barker and Ramsdell and Mr. Winkler, to gather the Southern historical collection, which is remarkable now and which promises to be marvelous later. That is his left hand. With his other hand he has presented to us the Wrenn Library of English and American literature from 1500 to 1900—a collection of rare and beautiful and great books which I know several other universities strove hard to secure, but which, thanks to the generosity of Major Littlefield, we have. In the two years since its purchase, its worth in mere dollars has increased, I believe, to more than three times the purchase price. It is a superb donation, one whose value will go on increasing. Three hundred years from now the gift will still be lauded as an "unspeakable benefit." Men are not numerous ever who possess both the great wealth and the imaginative vision to give so nobly and so well. To us of the present the gift is most grateful. It heartens us. Doubtless we need criticism. Assuredly we have had it. Even the criticism of ignorance and of malice is not without its value. But approbation *is* cheering, welcome as sunshine in winter. And he who extends a hand to help, wins our love and admiration.

The state by legislative appropriation has not been ungenerous. Funds supplied by it, expended as judiciously as they have been, would have provided a library to compare favorably with other Southern libraries—in Georgia, Kentucky, North Carolina, Virginia. But with the additions from individual citizens our library is placed far in advance of any other Southern library.

Let me narrow the basis of comparison. It is not quite fair to do so, for it shows us perhaps fairer and brighter than we really are. Take, however, one group of books as an index of the rest, and discount the comparison as you may please—the books printed in England up to the year 1640. This group includes Elizabethan literature. (Rich as the Wrenn Library is in these books, it is nevertheless still richer in the books of later years.) On Tuesday of this week I received a letter from the man in the best position to make comparisons. This is the sum of what he says: You fall considerably behind Yale and Harvard, but are a good deal ahead of the universities of Michigan, Minnesota, California, Chicago, Wellesley, Oberlin, and Vassar; in some respects you are the equal of, in some fall behind, Columbia.

The Huntington Library of California, not a college library at all, is in these books far superior to any other library whatever in America.

The East—Harvard and Yale considerably ahead of us. The West—California [Huntington] far ahead of us. Now complete the geographical triangle—the South. Texas leads and represents the South.

The South asks no man's pity. Yet she was maimed, and has been lame in the running. For long she has had to send the flower of her youth from home for the needed higher learning. Of late she begins to come more into her own. Now one of her sons gives into the hands of Texas as a trustee a treasure for the use and enrichment of all her sons and daughters.

When I sit in the Wrenn Library, I, too, feel as did old Heinsius: "In the very bosom of Eternity among all these illustrious souls I take my seat." There is magic there and high romance. To hold in my hand the very book that once belonged to Ben Jonson, see his name written by his own pen, in his own ink; or a book that Locke owned; or a manuscript of Izaak Walton, or Charlotte Brontë, or Edgar Allan Poe! There is beauty there. Many a binder has strained his art to clothe beautifully the body of a great thought. And there is adventure there, the greatest of all adventures—the discovering of something new, unknown before to the world. Already scholars have begun to seek us out. And they will come more and more.

Today we dedicate the Wrenn Library—this place of beauty, of romance, of adventure. And we dedicate it to the increase of knowledge, to research, to the finest adventure, the discovery of things new among men.

Am I too ambitious when I say that in this matter of books, as in all other matters, I want Texas to be as good as the best?

What is Texas? One hundred years ago Stephen F. Austin founded the colony in a wilderness. Last year the state paid into the national treasury in income and excess-profits taxes—just these two items alone—the sum of 62 millions of dollars. A territory stretching from El Paso to Texarkana, from Colorado to the Gulf, imperial in its vastness. A population of five million souls, where fifty millions yet will be. A soil and a sun pouring wealth lavishly into the lap of its citizenry. A people that is fitted to be and of right ought to be a leader among nations! Can you not see the state as a young giant, lithe and strong, deep-chested, shaking his shoulders and girding himself for his part in the race of the ages! A state and a people to rejoice in, to be proud of!

Hither from all quarters of the commonwealth, from all parts of this Texas of our loyalty and pride, come the sons and daughters of the people, come hither to the University in their youth to learn the best answer they may to the question, "What is the meaning of life? Why is it given to us? What shall we do with it, make of it?"

They are the chosen spirits. They are the master minds. Not the least among them but shall be a leader in his community in subsequent years. Hither they come, and at the altar of Alma Mater light and trim their torches and prepare to run their part in the Great Race. They come hither to the University as to a city that is set on a hill and cannot be hid; to the University, whose function, whose life is to find more of light, to spread among men the light which shall light the world onward; to the University, which must and shall be both prepared and determined to encourage, to cheer onward, to help forward and upward those who are "enflamed with the study of learning and the admiration of virtue; who are stirred up with high hopes of living to be brave men and worthy patriots, dear to God and famous to all ages."

But a race for the mere running profits nothing. No race without its goal! And this, the Great Torch Race up from the blackness of the night of ignorance—what is its goal? What is it but enlightenment? Enlightenment, which is Truth—that Truth which shall make us free. "The first creature of God, in the work of days, was the light of the sense; the last was the light of reason. First he breathed light upon the face of matter; then he breathed light into the face of man; and still he breatheth and inspireth light into the face of his chosen."

His "Chosen!" And may we not be his chosen if we so choose?

"Breatheth and inspireth light."

Light!

If you will take a beam of sunlight and cause it to fall upon a prism, you will have a very beautiful effect. The one ray will become a ribbon cross-banded with light—not white light any more, but all the colors of the rainbow. White light, then, contains within itself, or, better still, is composed of, all these colors, from violet through all shades to red. For these separate colors recombined make white light again—the perfect light.

In the Great Torch Race must be bearers of torches burning with all colors, not the great primary colors alone, but all the infinite gradations between them in the scale, and above and below them. Men are the bearers; the torches themselves are ideas. All the inventions we now have, all the discoveries that have been made, all the ideas we possess, all phases of knowledge, and all improvements upon them were once new, were born in some human brain, and, like torches passed from hand to hand, have been scattered among men. Saturn is fabled to have invented agriculture, and Cadmus the alphabet.

Prometheus was bringer of fire. Watts, Stephenson, Fulton, Morse, Bell, have curtailed space. Marconi puts a girdle around the earth more speedily than Puck in the play. Philosophers, musicians, poets, actors, prophets, discoverers, inventors, novelists, men who set law or government or business in a better way, each and all contribute a color or shade or tint to the sum of the whole.

When time shall come to its end, far yonder in the future, when the race shall have been run and the goal reached, and the number of torches shall be fulfilled, then the flames, the colors of all the torches that humanity carries, shall blend; and from them shall leap, shall be born, single and undivided, the white light of truth. In that day, when days shall cease and time shall be no more, then Man, freed from the shadows of darkness, bathed in beams of ineffable light, shall see God, whose dwelling from eternity to eternity is Light. In that Splendor may it not be found that we have lagged in the running, have left to any other hands the torches we might have borne.

REGINALD HARVEY GRIFFITH